Literary Freedom

a Cultural Right
to Literature

Literary Freedom

a Cultural Right to Literature

Heather Katharine McRobie

Winchester, UK
Washington, USA

First published by Zero Books, 2013
Zero Books is an imprint of John Hunt Publishing Ltd., Laurel House, Station Approach,
Alresford, Hants, SO24 9JH, UK
office1@jhpbooks.net
www.johnhuntpublishing.com
www.zero-books.net

For distributor details and how to order please visit the 'Ordering' section on our website.

Text copyright: Heather Katharine McRobie 2013

ISBN: 978 1 78099 880 0

A CIP catalogue record for this book is available from the British Library.

Design: Stuart Davies

Printed and bound by CPI Group (UK) Ltd, Croydon, CR0 4YY

We operate a distinctive and ethical publishing philosophy in all
areas of our business, from our global network of authors to
production and worldwide distribution.

CONTENTS

Introduction

The Warsaw Pact invasion of Czechoslovakia that followed the 1968 Prague Spring entailed numerous authoritarian restrictions by the new political forces. Among these were "purges [that] "cleansed" the Czech cultural scene of four hundred writers"[1] with the consequence that "at a stroke, the Czech cultural community - almost in its entirety - was removed from public life and become 'non persons'. Writers were the most affected."[2] Although the Warsaw Pact measures have become a symbol of some of the worst excesses of the oppression of writers under twentieth century authoritarian regimes, the phenomenon continues to be widespread, if not global: literary freedom organisation English PEN has documented 647 cases of attacks on writers, journalists, publishers and others in 2011 worldwide, noting that 53 writers and journalists were murdered due to their profession in 2007 alone.[3]

However, the encroachments on the civil liberties of writers described by historians looking at post-1968 Czechoslovakia, and the ongoing attacks enumerated by organisations such as PEN, sit alongside a recent event which highlights the complexity of the concept of freedom of literary expression: namely, that in April 2009 PEN Slovakia, an organisation which campaigns on behalf of persecuted writers and in favour of freedom of expression[4], issued a statement condemning the publication in a Slovakian journal of a poem by Radovan Karadžić, the wartime Bosnian Serb leader currently on trial for war crimes at the International Criminal Tribunal for the former Yugoslavia (ICTY).[5]

Although PEN Slovakia did not elaborate at length on the reasons behind their condemnation of the publication, it seems reasonable to assume that it was due to either, or both, Radovan Karadžić's role in genocide, war crimes and other grievous atrocities during the wars of the former Yugoslavia in the 1990s, or due to the ultranationalist content of the poetry itself, carrying with it the potential to incite ultranationalist violence. In any case, the incident – in which an organisation that campaigns for literary freedom called for, in effect, censorship – opens up the conundrums and unresolved tensions latent in the concept of "freedom of literary expression."

The argument I will outline in the following Chapters aims to demonstrate that these conundrums would be better resolved if we change the way we think about freedom of expression – and thus freedom of *literary* expression – by moving away from the traditional negative liberty approach that has thus far dominated the political philosophy consideration of freedom of expression, and towards a more proactive one, which can be built from the capabilities approach developed by Amartya Sen and Martha Nussbaum.

The questions these two cases – Czechoslovakia in 1968, and PEN Slovakia's condemnation of Karadžić's poetry forty years later –are highly germane to ongoing debates related to human rights theory, human rights in practice, and contemporary political philosophy. At first glance, the juxtaposition of these two cases brings to mind various interrelated questions, for instance: is literary freedom, then, only the absence of censorship? If this is the case then on what grounds, if any, is censorship of literary works justifiable? Is literary freedom substantively different from other forms of freedom of expression? Are the rights that writers enjoy the rights that belong to the general populace – civil and political rights, such as the right not to be tortured or arbitrarily detained and so forth – or do they also have rights *in their capacity as writers*? If so, are there corresponding duties that accompany these rights?

To address these issues, I will explore the concept of freedom of literary expression, in particular, by building upon and exploring potential points of departure with the traditional political philosophy debate regarding freedom of expression as a whole. Freedom of expression is classically read as a cornerstone of civil and political rights, enshrined in international law under Article 19 of the Universal Declaration of Human Rights.[6] Here, I aim to demonstrate, however, that freedom of literary expression is also a cultural right. Drawing upon Isaiah Berlin's delineation of negative and positive liberty, this book takes the position of the capabilities approach developed by Amartya Sen and Martha Nussbaum, that only a positive liberty approach that entails proactive steps on behalf of states can comprehensively secure the rights of all citizens. Conceiving of the right to literary expression as a cultural right entails a conceptual shift away from the classically liberal, negative liberty approach to freedom of expression, which has traditionally been defended by theorists like J. S. Mill solely in terms of the rights of the individual to freedom of expression.

Freedom of literary expression, when analysed through the lens of the capabilities approach, entails the protection not only of the individual writer to produce literature free from arbitrary governmental constraint, but also entails protecting the right of the wider group or community to access and enjoy literary culture. In other words, the drastic measures against writers in, for instance, post-1968 Czechoslovakia, should not merely be read as an encroachment on the civil and political rights of individual writers, but also a violation of the group rights of the community to enjoy culture.

The capabilities approach has not been fully applied to the question of literary freedom of expression. Consequently, making the case for literary expression as a cultural right entails drawing upon seemingly discrete academic traditions or debates. More specifically, here I will be addressing several questions that frequently arise in the debate on economic, social and cultural rights; I aim to synthesise answers to these questions, in order to demonstrate the validity of Sen and

Nussbaum's positive liberty position against both Rawlsian social contractarianism and utilitarianism. The first question which frequently arises in literature on economic, social and cultural rights – the question addressed in Chapter 1 – is "what is the importance of culture?" The second, more specific question, which frequently arises on the subject of cultural rights – and which I will address in Chapter 2 – is "should the state fund "high art"?" Chapter 3 will then bring these two concerns together through an analysis of the role of the writer in society, and the relationship between the writer and society, which underscores the central claim of the argument I am presenting here: that civil and political rights, and economic social and cultural rights, are mutually reinforcing, and cannot be fully secured independently of one another. Building upon Chapter 3's tentative recommendations for ways to address literary freedom of expression through the capabilities approach, Chapter 4 will deal with the remaining question of literary hate speech, primarily by focusing on the example of Radovan Karadžić's poetry, and present a way of addressing this thorny issue that moves beyond the impasses of the traditional/ negative liberty approach – namely, how to apply the capabilities approach to (literary) hate speech, to develop the position of "speaking back".

Taken together, these four Chapters will make the case that:

(a) literary freedom is a cultural right, entailing obligations on the part of the state and
(b) literary hate speech (addressed in Chapter 4) must similarly be approached through a positive liberty/ capabilites lens, also entailing positive actions such as "speaking back" rather than negative actions like censorship.

In other words, the work as a whole is an assertion of the importance and relevance of applying a positive liberty and capabilities approach to an issue that has traditionally been treated as a negative liberty or civil and political issue.

In keeping with this synthesis of different academic debates, the literature consulted for this book draws upon a number of different schools of thought, primarily in political philosophy, but also literary theory, social history, and constructivist approaches to nationalism. Although these different schools of thought, with their own internal debates and frameworks, may seem unrelated – and I recognise that this may at first seem like a disadvantage to the overall coherence of the argument – it is necessary to bring together these different academic traditions in order to make the case I am presenting here, of literary freedom as a cultural right, due to the fact that it is a notably underdeveloped part of human rights theory and political philosophy. Making the case that (*any*) freedom of expression should be addressed through the capabilities approach rather than a negative liberty approach would already have been a departure from the predominant way of understanding freedom of expression; focusing on literary freedom in particular, as I will in the following Chapters, makes the task doubly complicated, and thus entails bringing together diverse approaches to freedom of expression, rights theory, and literary theory.

Consequently, Chapter 1 draws upon both the constructivist approach to nationalism (to show how the contested concept of 'culture' has been appropriated and constructed by, among others, the ideology of nationalism) as well as the debate within political philosophy, namely the arguments of Waldron, Kymlicka and Young, who are delineating the potential conflicts between group rights and the rights of the individual, and present different theses on the importance of culture to individual identity/ individual freedom. Post-colonialist and post-structuralist thinkers such as Judith Butler, Gayatri Chakravorty Spivak and Homi Bhabha also provide insight into this question, as both are pointing to the "false neutrality" latent in Western (individual rights-based) multiculturalism, and provide salient analysis of the transgressive/ mutable element of culture.

Chapter 2 outlines the twentieth century debate within the Frankfurt School and its successors, notably Adorno's idea of the "culture industry", before outlining how Sen and Nussbaum's capabilities approach provides a more helpful lens for responding to those who argue "high art" should not be funded or receive other proactive support from the state and society as a whole, due to its latently elitist nature. Chapter 3 references the schools of thought outlined in the first two Chapters, and also draws upon commentators looking specifically at the role of the writer in society, such as Achebe's essay 'The Role of the Writer in a New Nation', and Orwell's insights on literary self-censorship, then using the case of writers in post-1968 Czechoslovakia to highlight the importance of taking proactive steps to ensure freedom of literary expression.

Turning to the question of literary hate speech, and how this can be dealt with through the capabilites approach, Chapter 4 will first draw upon work by scholars looking at Radovan Karadžić's poetry, and those who seek to locate this within the broader construction of Serbian ultranationalism, and then turn to analysis of other works of what could be termed artistic 'hate speech', such as Sontag's analysis of the Nazi film-maker Leni Riefenstahl, to clarify the findings of the Chapter: that literary hate speech must be contextualised to strip it of its power, and that positive steps must be taken to counteract it, such as Gelber's proposal (following Nussbaum) of a forum for disadvantaged groups to "speak back". All Chapters reference the capabilities approach developed by Sen and Nussbaum.

In addition to these schools of thought or literature, three cases in particular will be foregrounded in this study in order to more fully explore the question of literary freedom, its limits, and what it entails. They each serve to highlight a different aspect of the debate. The first, as stated above, is the oppression of writers in post-1968 Czechoslovakia and the impact that this had not merely on the individual writers but also on the society as a whole, which highlights the way in which literary freedom is not solely a civil and political right. The second is the case of Radovan Karadžić's poetry, which highlights the dilemma of the limits of freedom of literary expression and provides an opportunity to demonstrate the capability approach's appropriateness for solving this traditionally negative liberty dilemma. (To this, we could add the example of Leni Riefenstahl who, although not a literary figure, is relevant to this analysis because Susan Sontag's reading of her work, and its place in society, is also vital to the argument I am making, regarding 'contextualisation' as an alternative to censorship). The third case that I will return to throughout this exploration is that of Salman Rushdie, and the persecution he received for the publication of his novel *The Satanic Verses*. Rushdie is included as a counter-point to Riefenstahl and Karadžić, to demonstrate that we need an approach to hate speech that can distinguish between the offence caused by *The Satanic Verses* on the one hand and the tangible harm caused by Karadžić's poetry (and Riefenstahl's art) on the other. Moreover, the case of Salman Rushdie was also taken up as one of the key examples through which the ongoing debate in contemporary political philosophy and multicultural theory – the debate between Brian Barry, Bikhu Parekh, Kymlicka and others – played itself out. As I intend to take on board, but ultimately refute, Brian Barry's egalitarian critique of 'group rights' leveled against Parekh, the Rushdie case is a particularly fitting example.

I will not discuss the artistic merit of the literary works in question, on the principle that artistic merit should not enter into the discussion of freedom of expression and art.[7] Similarly, it was beyond the remit of this exploration to engage in close textual analysis of Karadžić's poetry in order to fully demonstrate the way in which it functions as 'hate speech', and I have largely relied upon other scholars' analysis of his poetry to make this case.

It should be noted here that art (here, literature) has often been overlooked in debates on freedom of expression, and yet art and literature have frequently been effectively utilised by fascistic, ultranationalist and other extremist regimes to stoke social violence. Hate speech in art is a sensitive issue with tangible consequences, and part of my intention with the analysis of literary hate speech in Chapter 4 was driven from my position that literary hate speech cannot be adequately dealt with through a self-satisfied liberal reaction that simply recites its commitment to free speech in the face of disadvantaged groups who object to literature that incites violence against them. The affront Karadžić's poetry and Riefenstahl's films cause to those affected by the crimes of the respective regimes to which they were aligned is real and undeniable, and any conclusion on the side of allowing the transmission of hate speech in art and literature – as I am ultimately making – must not lose sight of this fact.

As this work intends to demonstrate the advantages of a capabilities approach to freedom of expression (one that has not been developed in the literature on capabilities theory, except for Katherine Gelber's study, and which has not been applied to literary freedom of expression in particular) – and particularly its advantages over the more established political philosophy lens for dealing with freedom of expression – the remaining part of the Introduction will outline first the 'traditional' way in which freedom of expression has been dealt with by political philo-sophers and liberal theorists, and then outline the capabilities approach, which in the following Chapters I hope to show offers new insights and ways beyond the impasses of the traditional approach.

Freedom of Expression

Freedom of expression is a central, fiercely-guarded tenet of liberal thought, and grounds for overriding it requires convincing justification.[8] Here I will first illustrate why freedom of expression is central to liberal philosophy, then demonstrate that which *cannot* be considered grounds for censorship, namely offensiveness. This leaves the issue of free speech which causes harm to others, an area where traditional political philosophy is less helpful than on offense. (It is worth noting that one of the problems with the traditional debate – perhaps a sign of its Western, academic origins – is that it often chooses as examples for the 'free speech dilemma' issues such as pornography, vulgarity and practical examples, like the ethics of the freedom to shout "fire" in a crowded theatre, from which it is not easy to find serious equivalences with the grave effects of ultranationalist/fascistic hate speech, namely incitement to genocide, warcrimes and social violence

Freedom of expression is so universally accepted as an inherent good in liberal philosophy that it almost seems strange to ask *why* it is important.

Several overlapping reasons have been put forth by political philosophers working in this area. The first comes from the utilitarian tradition of J.S. Mill, and is grounded in the concept of negative liberty, which asserts that every person has the liberty to do or say anything provided it does not harm others, and there can be no legitimate interference with the exercise of this liberty. Secondly, Joseph Raz has argued that free speech is an essential public good, as it is only when free speech is guaranteed that individuals can participate in their broader cultures/groups, which is essential for personal identity.[9] A related argument is the necessity of free speech for democracy, which David Richards describes as "protection of the democratic political process from the abusive censorship of political debate by the transient majority."[10]

A final argument is that free speech is an inherent social good because it is a catalyst for debate, leading to new ideas which help society as a whole. Historically linked to the Liberal/Whig idea of progress, this idea is often cited to defend free expression in academia. Even if much freedom of expression does not contribute to progress, there is no way to know whether it will unless we allow a culture of free speech to flourish. Taken together, these arguments indicate that, if we are ever to override the principle of freedom of expression, we are compelled to provide good reasons for doing so.[11]

One reason sometimes cited for overriding free speech is the ground of offensiveness. Liberal theorists have clearly shown that such a principle is untenable. Enshrined in national laws in many liberal democracies, there have been numerous cases in recent history where this argument was presented by/ in the name of social groups, often disadvantaged groups who face discrimination in wider society. The argument can be summarised thus: although free speech is a right, it cannot be abused to gratuitously offend peoples' deeply-held beliefs or morality. This argument was used against Salman Rushdie's *The Satanic Verses*, which was deemed by several Muslim (and Christian) organisations to be insulting to Islam, and therefore causing harm to Muslims.

Crucially, however, Rushdie's novel, which depicted historical-religious figures important to Islam, did not incite violence to Muslims or any social group – even those who argued that his work should be banned did not base their claim on 'incitement to racial hatred.'[12] It is true that *The Satanic Verses* violated edicts of Islam according to many rigorous interpretations, but Rushdie's book does not constitute hate speech by being 'blasphemous' to one religion: to critique or parody an idea that is important to others does not in itself incite discrimination or violence. In fact, we can even argue the reverse: blasphemy laws, which continue to be in place countries including Ireland and Canada, unjustifiably oppress individuals' right to free speech.

That offence is not harm coheres with our common sense: people can be 'offended' at innocuous things like an interracial couple holding hands, a gay couple kissing and so on.[13] Grounds for offence are often spurious, and, if religion is cited as a reason, how can we logically justify religion jumping to the front of the queue? After all, why is it more of an affront if it offends my religion than if it offends my belief in liberty? So if we are to restrict free speech on certain grounds, it surely must be on stronger grounds than offensiveness. It could be argued that part of the lack of validity of claims of 'offensiveness' is its closeness to, and ability to act as a veil for, the feeling of "disgust" as offensiveness/ cultural and religious taboos are often developed out of and closely linked to ideas of what society deems "disgusting" and this disgust is then given a veneer of legitimacy under the auspices of "culture".

Martha Nussbaum, for instance, has argued that the concepts of disgust and shame are inherently hierarchical, and have historically been used to oppress the disadvantaged in Western society, particularly women, homosexuals and Jews. She concludes that disgust can never be a legitimate reason to curtail another person's liberty.

Some conclude, in the face of examples like the Rushdie controversy, that we should not have any restrictions on freedom of expression. The libertarian response is to note that all attempts at restriction are open to abuse, of plaintiffs who are excessively sensitive or misconstrue the concept of harm in order to silence others. Linked to the broader libertarian view that intervention in an individual's practices is to be avoided as much as possible, it is also tied to the question of "who will censor the censors?" If the state – or the 'moral majority' – appoints itself as the arbitrator of when freedom of speech be restricted on the grounds of harm, then the state or majority will likely define harm as that which goes against their interests or diminishes their power.

Yet this position does not entirely hold up to scrutiny either. Jan Narveson starts from the libertarian position that everyone has the right to say what they like. But he then shows how this raises the question of whether there is a corresponding right to be heard, as speech is usually done "to" someone, and yet 'noise pollution' – speech we do not want to hear, yet find hard to avoid for practical reasons – would infringe on our liberties. If we have a right to liberty *from* excessive noise pollution in everyday life, it creates a corresponding restriction of free speech on those who produce noise pollution.[14]

Secondly, Narveson raises the issue of third parties: the initial libertarian formulation of 'right to say what we like' does not consider the issue beyond the intended audience: whether A's speech to B has harmful effects on C. Yet this is how much hate speech functions, and defending the liberty of C would necessitate restrictions on the liberty of A and B.[15]

Narveson also raises the question of 'culpable inducement[16']: if A's speech compels B to assault C, is it the fault of A or B? In other words, even if we can demonstrate that there are limits on freedom of expression on the grounds of harm, the question of where to lay the blame for the harm it causes becomes the obstacle.

The positions outlined above highlight the limitations of the traditional debate. Those who argue there should be no limits are absolutising free speech as a first virtue, not fully acknowledging the negative impacts this has on other important social virtues like equality and justice. Conversely, those in favour of censorship when free speech harms others are overly-focused on 'explicit' hate speech and where to apportion blame. In liberal discourse, the language of "striking a balance" dominates analysis of where to draw the line of free speech: the goal – to diminish the harm hate speech causes – is juxtaposed with the principle of upholding as much free speech as possible. As long as these two 'rights' or 'goods' are seen to be in conflict, there can be no comprehensive solution – we will forever be adjusting the scales between these concerns. As Chapter 4 will go on to show, it is only by moving beyond a negative liberty focus, and drawing upon Nussbaum's capabilities approach, that we can find a solution in which these two goals and principles are not problematically juxtaposed.

In conclusion, although we can assert that offense is not adequate grounds for overriding free speech, little can be determined beyond this, particularly as the traditional debate is not generally concerned with hate speech and its extreme potential consequences, and when it does it deals only with explicit incitements. As Chapter 4 will go on to demonstrate, the traditional debate's emphasis on explicit and overt hate speech makes it particularly ill-suited to art.

The Capabilities Approach

As Sen and Nussbaum's work provides the framework for my argument that literary freedom is a cultural right, it is worth now briefly outlining the capabilities approach, and its advantages over other contemporary theories of justice. Focused on securing "substantive freedoms" that have a meaningful impact on a person's full exercise of their choice (and thus, their ability to lead a fulfilled life of their own choosing), the capabilities approach differs from utilitarianism and Rawlsian social contractarianism, which maintain that civil and political rights can be secured before, and independently of, economic, social and cultural rights.[17] Instead, it argues that substantive freedom is achieved only by securing a core of key entitlements, such as resources, education, bodily integrity and the ability to live to an old age. These substantive freedoms allow people to pursue their own goals of fulfilment: in this sense, it is an outcome-oriented theory of justice, which measures the justness of any social arrangement or state by the extent to which it secures for each individual a list of central "capabilities", although these capabilities are also interdependent.

Moreover, each core entitlement is (though interdependent on the others for the development of an individual's freedom) an inalienable rights-claim in its own respect, thus it is not permissible — as has often been the case in modern states – to, for instance, justify the restriction of civil and political rights by rewarding citizens with economic development or greater social equality. It is a positive liberty approach inasmuch as it predicates the concept of freedom on the idea of meaningful choice, and seeks to enable all individuals to have as wide a choice as possible, seeking to mitigate against what economics have identified as "adaptive preferences."[18] The core entitlements identified by Sen and Nussbaum belong, in their theory, to 'humanity in general', and thus there is a positive obligation and moral imperative on the part of states (and, Nussbaum suggests in her work on transnational justice, to other bodies who wield state-like power) to secure these entitlements to all inhabitants of their state.

As the claim to entitlement is a moral, rights-based claim, it would – in keeping with human rights mechanisms –also be inadmissible for a state to only secure them for their citizens as opposed to all who inhabit the state's borders.

In international mechanisms, the capabilities approach is most closely linked to the UN's Human Development Index. In addition, the capabilities approach has several tools in international law that construct the case – as I will do in the following Chapters – that literary freedom is a positive cultural right. As noted above, Article 19 of the UDHR provides the legal basis for freedom of literary expression as a civil and political right exercised by individual writers. In addition to this, there are important tools in each of the two UN Covenants that followed the UDHR. The first is Article 27 of the International Covenant on Civil and Political Rights, which claims – in purely individual-rights, and negative or non-interventionist terms – that minorities not be denied the right (amongst other things) to enjoy their own culture.

Article 27 thus brings up both the right to "culture" and acknowledges the concept of the "group" (or the minority), but does not entail any positive obligations on the part of states to actively secure this right through their actions. On the other hand, Article 15 of the International Covenant of Economic, Social and Cultural Rights asserts the right to take part in cultural life, and "the benefits to be derived from the encouragement and development of international contacts and co-operation in the scientific and cultural fields."

Although Article 15 of the ICESCR is not specifically asserting a positive right and thus obligations on the part of the state to secure the right to access and participate in culture, it does show traces of the shift towards seeing economic, social and cultural rights as goals that states should aim to progressively achieve, using the best of their available resources. Moreover, as the concept of the "right to participate in culture" clearly echoes Sen and Nussbaum's view that substantive freedoms must be secured by enabling true access and participation, not merely through state abstention from persecution and the denial of civil and political rights.

As the capabilities approach is holistic, recognising that all rights must be secured simultaneously for any to be meaningfully enjoyed, this entails that securing the various rights enshrined in the ICCPR and the ICESCR are necessary to secure – in the case of my argument here – literary freedom; Article 13 of the ICESCR, asserting the right to education, is particularly relevant in this case. Lastly, it is worth noting that the interdependence of "first" and "second" generation rights, which the capabilities approach asserts, has also been mirrored in international legal procedures, notably at the Vienna Conference of 1993, which asserted that the rights protected in turn by each of the Covenants are interrelated.

Although it is often dismissed as a minor concern of the cultural elite, the suppression of writers is not only a violation of the civil and political rights of the individual writer, but also a violation of the broader community's right to fully enjoy and participate in cultural life. As the following Chapters will argue, the symbiotic relationship between the writer and society is a prism through which the interrelated nature of "first" and "second" generation rights is illuminated.

In addition to this general point, which the capabilities approach asserts – that civil and political rights cannot be secured before, or independently of, economic, social and cultural rights – my aim is to demonstrate that the writer as a social figure is also of particular concern, as writers and artists play a role in fostering the moral imagination of society, and it is this moral imagination – or, as Nussbaum has identified, the interrelated forces of rationality and empathy – from which human rights values emerge. The following Chapters will outline how literary freedom is a cultural right, entailing obligations on the part of the state and consequently how literary hate speech must similarly be approached through the positive liberty lens of the capabilities approach, also entailing positive actions such as "speaking back" rather than negative actions like censorship.

Chapter 1

Culture as a Group Right

To begin to make the case that literary freedom of expression is a cultural right, this Chapter will address the concept of what a cultural right entails, bearing in mind the debates on freedom of expression outlined in the Introduction. This Chapter will advance the argument that cultural rights have a necessarily group rights component, whilst recognising the critiques that theorists such as Waldron and Barry have made against group rights. This is tied to the larger project of my argument: to demonstrate that literary freedom of expression is a cultural right requires we understand what a cultural right comprises, and how it must be upheld.

To make this case, this Chapter will explore various debates – the first relates to the concept of "culture" itself, particularly the insights that scholars looking at nationalism from a constructivist viewpoint can bring to this issue; the second relates to the internal divisions and ongoing conversation within multicultural theory amongst thinkers such as Kymlicka, Waldron and I.M. Young; the third relates to the additional insights that theorists such as Gayatri Chakravorty Spivak and Judith Butler, who are looking at the 'transgressive' element in culture, can bring to the discussion of group rights and their tension with individual liberty. The subsequent Chapters will build upon and refer back to the analysis presented here.

1.1 The contested notion of 'culture'

In order to sustain the position that literary freedom entails cultural rights, it is necessary to first demonstrate that there is a legitimate case for cultural rights, which are by necessity in some sense group rights, and thus not part of the classical liberal conception of human rights solely as political and civil rights that individuals exercise independently. It goes without saying, however, that the concept of "culture" is itself highly contested, and countless definitions have been offered from cultural anthropologists, historians, sociologists and so on.[19] Instead of ennumerating the myriad ways in which culture has been conceived and debated by scholars, let us start from a common sense observation of the everyday use of the word "culture": in the English language, at least, the word has two separate predominant connotations, one relating to everyday customs, tradition, and practices ('Innuit culture', 'Montenegrin culture', and subcultures, such as 'punk culture'), and one relating to what could be called capital-C Culture, that is, the arts (for instance the Culture section of a European broadsheet newspaper will encompass reviews of ballet, opera, literary fiction, cinema and so on). Another way of phrasing this has traditionally been a dichotomy between "high culture" and "low culture".

However – and this is one potential inroad into a better understanding of some of the facets of this contested word – the interplay between high and low culture, or culture and Culture, is itself highly dynamic, as scholars such as Hobsbawm, Anderson and Gellner, taking a constructivist approach to nationalism, have highlighted. (Though the construction of nations and nationalism is by no means the only prism through which to unpick the concept of "culture", it is particularly relevant here as it touches upon issues of power, false 'authenticity' and exclusivist constructions of identity, all of which underpin the following debates in this study).

All three scholars highlight, amongst other things, the power dynamics behind claims to "culture", the way in which the concept of "culture" was utilised during the constructions of European nationalism in the eighteenth and nineteenth century to generate exclusivist identities demarcating an "us" and "them" along constructed ethnic, religious, national (that is, "cultural") lines, and that so-called "high art" facilitated this process of construction through its appropriation of and interplay with the supposedly 'authentic' culture of the people or 'Volk'.

In his study *Imagined Communities*, Anderson charts the trajectory of conceptions of nationalism and the nation-state from the early modern period to the post-colonial era, positing that nationalism should be viewed as a "cultural artefact"[20] of various social trends (rather than, as a primordialist interpretation of nationalism would posit, as something "natural" and immutable). In particular, Anderson pinpoints the emergence of the imagined communities which underpin modern nationalism to the twinned developments of print-capitalism and Protestantism in Europe (with its emphasis on the vernacular language, rather than Church Latin), which laid the foundations for people to conceptualise their relations to one another, and beyond their immediate sphere of daily contact, in entirely new ways, which created new modes of identity. In particular, print-capitalism and the proliferation of printing combined with nascent urbanisation (although it preceded industrialisation) to give provincial and peripheral elites in large multilingual empires such as the Habsburg empire a newfound awareness of their disadvantaged position vis-a-vis the elite of the imperial centre, and this awareness brought forth a desire amongst provincial elites to construct their own identities.

Parallel to this, the codification and standardisation of languages necessitated by the emergence of mass printing fed into the creation of more clearly defined conceptions of the boundaries of comprehensibility of language, rather than a continuum of dialects, and these new, print-made linguistic boundaries helped construct the idea of (among other things, *linguistically*-based) "nations" as discrete entities.

Moreover, most crucially to the exploration I am undertaking here, Anderson outlines how this process led the literate provincial elites to reconceptualise their relationship with the illiterate peasants with whom, as they were increasingly aware, they shared a common language, and thus share an identity: across Europe, the provincial elites engaged in acts of reclaiming (through in reality it was construction rather than reclamation) the cultural customs, folklore, arts and traditions of provincial peasants. These adopted and reappropriated aspects of 'Volk' or peasant culture became entrenched, and treated as ahistorical, immutable natural artefacts of the nascent nations or imagined communities, by the elites who elevated them to symbols of their nation's heritage. Among the methods through which this was done was through the simultaneous fetishisation of the "natural" 'folk customs' by the elite and their sanitisation and standardisation through (written) high art, such as the collections of 'folk tales' collected by the Brothers Grimm and Vuk Karadžić, and the standardised folk music of early ethnomusicologists such as Bartók.

To Anderson's analysis, Hobsbawm and Ranger[21] hone in on the construction of European nationalism, and its dynamic relation between folk culture and high art, by following the thread of "invented traditions" particularly in the Romantic reaction to the Enlightenment. In *Invented Traditions*, a predominant theme is the search for, and false construction of, authentic culture, amongst intellectuals and artists in the eighteenth and nineteenth century, in order to generate a shared history of a nation. For instance, the study details how the modern idea of the Scottish kilt, initially developed in large part out of a parade for the benefit of English Georgian royalty, became reappropriated as a symbol of (ancient) Scottishness, and a symbolic marker against the Anglo-Saxons to the south.

Similarly, theorists who wish to point to the constructed nature of modern nationalism, and its falsely authentic acts of myth-making point to the case of the "Scottish Homer" Ossian, which Hobsbawm and Ranger's volume describes as an elaborate forgery by the eighteenth century writer James Macpherson, who wrote and then claimed to discover an ancient epic poem in Scots Gaelic, which was rapturously received by contemporary intellectuals as proof of Scotland's ancient and noble heritage. As Hobsbawm outlines, such acts of invented tradition often predicated their claims to legitimacy on the value of the authenticity – and ancientness – of cultural practices and artefacts, even as they were necessarily codified and transmitted through modern means and shaped to fit contemporary bourgeois sensibilities.

Although there is not space here to fully outline the many implications of the constructivist reading of nationalism sketched above, it is worth pointing out that one overriding theme in the analysis of Anderson, Hobsbawm, Gellner and others, is the appropriation of "popular"culture by high culture, and the way in which, through this manner, the concepts of "culture" and "Culture" in Western thought developed in tandem to one another, both cultural artefacts of the same social processes. This dynamic should be borne in mind throughout the analysis in the following Chapters, which tends for the purpose of argument to treat "culture" and "Culture" (or "high art") each in turn, but should not be read as an assertion that these two categories are discrete and immutable.

Secondly, as will be demonstrated in Chapter 4's consideration of the poetry of Radovan Karadžić, such constructions of nationalism are necessarily bordered constructions, which through their elevation of a (mythical, pure) 'Volk' culture position the nation in hierarchical dominance against the 'Other', generating an exclusivist identity that hides within it the potential for antagonism, and worse, with those placed outside the boundary of the nation.

1.2 The right to culture and the concept of 'group rights'
And yet – constructed, manipulated, highly contested, and mutable though it may be – we nonetheless have a right to

culture, at least inasmuch as this is enshrined in international legal documents such as the International Covenant on Economic, Social and Cultural Rights. Moreover, the central claim of my work here is that we have a right to *literary* culture, which entails positive actions on the part of states. How then do we assert the importance of culture without playing into the hands of those who – as Anderson, Hobsbawm and others have shown – seek to build or reinforce exclusivist identities through a construction of false authenticity, with its concomitant generation of a sharp and hostile definition of "us" and "them"?

Whilst some theorists will argue that this cannot be done, I believe that the case of the importance of culture – and the right to culture as a group right – can be asserted whilst avoiding this pitfall.

Here, I will argue the case for the validity of cultural rights of the kind enshrined in the International Convention on Economic, Social and Cultural Rights, and the necessity of their group dimension, by first presenting Waldron's classically liberal argument, before refuting this using arguments by Bhabha and Kymlicka. I.M. Young's contribution, which links cultural rights – and the necessity of group-identities – to a defence against oppression, presents a development to both Waldron's and Kymlicka's positions. Finally, recent scholars such as Gayatri Chakravorty Spivak and Judith Butler have further modified I. M. Young's position by demonstrating how trangressive/subversive voices are a crucial part *of* culture, which is a helpful improvement on the usual impasse – such as the impasse between Brian Barry and Bikhu Parekh – over the idea that group rights will be used to oppress individuals' rights and quell dissenting voices. As I will be constructing the case for group rights in Chapter 1, it is not possible to fully explore all aspects of these theorists' arguments, but only provide a brief overview of the debates.

For the purposes of the argument here, it could be said that "culture" here is a shorthand for culture in the sense of everyday practices, customs, and so on (whilst not disregarding the insight of Hobsbawm, Anderson and Ranger outlined above). It should be noted that, whilst mutlicultural theorists such as Waldron, Young and Kymlicka are predominantly addressing questions relating to 'minority culture' in the modern nation state, my concern is not with minority culture *per se*, and instead with the right to culture in general, in order to use this as a basis for a 'right to literary culture'.

However, it could be said that it is through the analysis of minority culture, and minorities' claims to cultural rights upon the nation state, that the conceptional paradigms related to the idea of a 'right to culture' – minority or predominant – have developed, as it is the presence of minorities in the modern nation state, and the minority-state relationship, that gave birth to the concept of "culture" as we understand it.

To begin with one proposal for addressing minorities and their right to culture, Jeremy Waldron presents a liberal case for assimilationist cosmopolitanism, in which individual rights are fully protected within a "kaleidoscope of cultures"[22] that exist together against the neutral backdrop of liberal democracy. For Waldron, group rights protecting an individual's culture of origin are unnecessary and may detract from the individual's right to fully exert their own civil/political rights. Waldron challenges the idea that cultures are homogenous entities – entailing, in turn, that they ought not to be protected. Through a description of a cosmopolitan metropolis in which many foods, musics, and other cultural aspects from across the world can comfortably mix, Waldron challenges the idea of "authenticity", which he claims the defence of groups rights is predicated upon. Any attempt to preserve culture as an entity in and of itself entails a false assumption of "authenticity", and does not recognise that all cultural "traditions" are contested and constantly changing: to preserve "culture" would therefore lead to stagnation, and oppress the individual (from within the 'traditional' culture) and their right to freely choose how to identify. Cosmopolitanism in liberal democracy, on the other hand, allows cultures, in their multiplicity, to thrive in a kind of marketplace of ideas, in which individuals from many different 'cultures of origin' assert their agency in choosing which aspects of their culture(s) to practice or keep.

Waldron's optimism, however, leaves him open to various criticisms. There is a false neutrality in Waldron's essay that fails to acknowledge global power dynamics, and which could in turn be seen as an assertion of privilege, or what Homi Bhabha has described as 'elite cosmopolitanism.'[23] Whilst Waldron's position rightly argues against the fetishisation of "authenticity", which is based on the false assumption that cultures are monolithic, fully-boundaried entities, Waldron's portrayal of cosmopolitanism is guilty of the same Orientalist/ essentialist fallacy, inasmuch as it presents the cosmopolitan alternative (in reality, found in the 'metropole', or, in different terms, the traditional 'colonial centre' of the West) as the sole crucible or melting-pot in which cultures meet.

The "cultural heterogeneity"[24] Waldron espouses implies that the rest of the world consists of monolithic, ahistorical 'cultures' that require the Western model of cosmopolitanism for them to come into contact with one another. This implication that non-Western/ non-"cosmopolitan" cultures are homogenous and static also has a temporal dimension, as the emergence of the "global community"[25] came, in Waldron's description, at the West's instigation, and occurs on their territory, time, and terms.

Building on Edward Said's analysis, Homi Bhabha argues against this 'elite cosmopolitanism' with the idea of the "third space"[26] in which the global subaltern (or, at least, the non-elite) navigate modernity without reference to this colonial/Western metropolitan "centre" and it is instead through this process that cultures continue to adapt, intersect, and exchange ideas and values. Bhabha's criticism is a helpful lens for highlighting the significant failures of Waldron's argument, but it does not in itself provide a comprehensive counter-argument to Waldron's thesis: working within post-colonial critical theory, Bhabha does not intend to present a political philosophy on the question of group rights and culture. For an alternative approach, it is helpful to turn to Kymlicka's argument, which survives Waldron's critique of it because, as demonstrated above, Waldron's own argument has several significant flaws.

Kymlicka asserts the necessity of the group component for individual identity, and thus individual freedom. Kymlicka notes that cultural contexts determine individuals' choices, and thus liberals such as Waldron "should be concerned with the fate of cultural structures, not because they have some moral status of their own, but because it's only through having a rich and secure cultural structure that people can become aware, in a vivid way, of the options available to them, and intelligently examine their value."[27]

To leave the cultures of national minorities to the marketplace of ideas in liberal democratic cosmopolitanism would entail the depletion of the "rich and secure cultural structure", and thus limit the capacity of individuals from the minority culture to fully exercise their freedom. The marketplace of ideas implicit in Waldron's seemingly neutral cosmopolitanism would in fact entail preference of the dominant group; not allowing for struc-tural accommodation of minorities (such as, for instance, allowing members of minority religions to take religious holidays, or have places of worship in public institutions) would keep them on the periphery of society.

Kymlicka's analysis also highlights a further drawback in Waldron's thesis, which presents the 'cosmopolitan alternative' as an emancipation from the confines of cultural-determinism, asserting that people don't *need* to 'belong' to one traditionally-defined culture. In doing so, Waldron fails to address the issue of *why* people choose to belong, or choose to retain or reaffirm their allegiance to one culture in particular. As Kymlicka highlights, this is because people can gain a feeling of individual emancipation through cultural belonging, not merely, as Waldron indicates, through embracing the 'cosmopolitan alternative'.

To Kymlicka's argument, I. M. Young's analysis of the politics of difference adds an important component: the power dynamics of majority/ minority cultures. Young delineates between assimilationist and diversity models of multiculturalism, and challenges what she describes as the "assimilationist ideal"[28] in which it is assumed that equal social status of different groups is assured by treating them all in the same way. Whilst assimilation of minority or disadvantaged groups (such as ethnic minorities, women, and sexual minorities) into the 'mainstream' may have the intention of achieving equality, emancipating these groups from their disadvantaged/ marginalised social position, Young demonstrates instead that this kind of equality entails a reiteration of the validity of the culture/ identity of the dominant group, which minorities or disadvantaged groups are merely being allowed to *join*.

Assimilation that ignores difference, such as "gender-blind" policies, actually disadvantage the non-privileged group[29] as bringing the disadvantaged into the mainstream on the mainstream's terms devalues the notion of belonging to other groups, reinforcing the "double consciousness" of the marginalised, who internalise the hierarchical values/ norms of the dominant.

Embracing the positivity of group difference, on the other hand, revokes this "double consciousness" through which dominant social groups have long held power, as it entails that members of minority/ disadvantaged groups reclaim "the identity that the dominant culture has taught them to despise."[30] When group difference is publicly and positively asserted, it relativises the dominant culture, making the differences between groups relational rather than hierarchical. This relativisation, Young argues, is the key to overcoming exclusion, and can only be achieved through the assertion of 'group belonging' by the minority/ disadvantaged group.

Young and Kymlicka's defence of the group protection of minority/ disadvantaged culture and identity unpicks much of the false neutrality of Waldron's depiction of the 'cosmopolitan alternative', and presents a coherent case for group rights. It should be noted, however, that classically liberal theorists such as Brian Barry could still argue, against Kymlicka and Young, that the institutional protection of minority cultures does still entail a 'boundary issue', presenting difficulties to the question of the self-identity of group members, and leading to the possibility that individuals who are publicly marked as 'belonging' to a minority group, and who transgress the norms/ cultural practices of that group, are oppressed in order to preserve the minority 'culture' as a whole.

In other words, the protection of minority rights merely shifts the problem of exclusion down to the level of the 'minority within the minority', or the individual within the minority. Barry and Waldron both take Salman Rushdie as a clear example of the abuse of 'group rights' to oppress an individual: from their viewpoint, it could be argued that, if minority culture – such as, for instance, the Muslim minority in Britain – is to be 'protected' (rather than assimilated) by the dominant culture, this entails protecting cultural practices that the majority (or self-appointed 'minority spokespeople') of the minority claim are integral to their culture.

If an individual who the 'spokespersons' claim is 'from' this minority culture (for instance, Rushdie appears to self-identify as an atheist humanist, but his 'culture of origin' is taken by some to be 'Indian Muslim', as well as belonging to British society) breaks the cultural practices/ norms of this culture, then the group-rights model would entail that this individual be silenced, to protect the practices of the group. The Rushdie case presents an impasse between two imperfect solutions: the false neutrality of Waldron's elite cosmopolitanism, or the group-right provisions of Kymlicka and Young, which consequently lead to stifling 'dissenting' members who are labelled as part of that group.

1.3 Transgressive voices: a way beyond the 'individual rights' vs 'group rights' impasse?

There are, however, ways around this dilemma between individual rights and group rights, which can allow us to assert the right to (literary) culture without committing us to the denigration of the rights of the individual. In particular, Judith Butler and Gayatri Chakravorty Spivak present an argument about the "performative" nature of identity, which can be used to modify Young and Kymlicka's analysis so that it does not face this pitfall. Butler and Spivak's exploration in *Who Sings The Nation State?* is largely in keeping with Young's critique of assimilationist policies such as "gender blindness", but it adds insight on the central role of "transgressive voices." While almost all academics working on multiculturalism and group rights seem to note the dilemma of the 'cultural boundary', in *Who Sings The Nation State?*, Spivak and Butler move the debate forward by arguing that the transgressive voice – such as, in my interpretation, Rushdie's 'voice' within the various 'communities' that others claim he belongs to – is an integral element of culture itself.

They take as an example the idea of singing the American national anthem in Spanish[31] to demonstrate – as others have argued – that culture is mutable, historical, and internally-diverse; it could be added, in turn, that this diversity, in itself, is what forms the core of each 'culture'. This resolves the problem of the 'group boundary', as it asserts that heterogeneity is a *defining* feature – not merely of the elite-cosmopolitanism 'multiculturalism' that Waldron describes – but of any notion of belonging; it is built into the very fabric of each culture. A sense of belonging to a 'group' thus entails a sense of belonging or affinity to a group of divergent voices – such as, for instance, the divergent and opposing voices of the rationalist secular Enlightenment and anti-Enlightenment Romanticism that *together* form a part of the history of 'Western' culture.

Whilst Parekh argued that the publication *The Satanic Verses* entailed an assertion of dominance over a disadvantaged group (and outlined the concept of 'group libel' as a defence against this), Barry responded by noting that Parekh's proposal would give self-defined 'groups', falsely claiming the authority of homogeneity, tools to unjustly oppress individuals who they labelled to be a member of their group – such as Rushdie being labelled a member of the Muslim community and therefore subject to the rulings of self-appointed 'moral spokespersons' within that community. Although Barry's argument against Parekh's idea of 'group libel' is convincing, this Chapter builds the argument that Barry's assertion of individual rights as the preserve of egalitarianism is not the final word in the debate, as incorporating Butler and Spivak's idea of the transgressive element within culture allows us to construct a pro-group rights position that nonetheless mitigates against the oppression of individuals. In other words, if we incorporate Butler's insights, we can both protect 'culture' as a group right and Rushdie's right to publish *The Satanic Verses*.

Read again through this lens, Rushdie's *The Satanic Verses* is not an aberration of 'Muslim culture', but part of the dialogue within the culture (and, simultaneously, part of the dialogue of the 'Western' literary canon), and it is through dissenting voices that culture is renewed, as an eternal, ongoing dialogue.

Adding this emphasis to Young's schema allows us to assert the importance of group rights, whilst countering Brian Barry and Waldron's liberal/ individualistic warning against the harm done when 'culture' or 'the group' is elevated above the individual. In short, it leads us to an understanding of culture as a macrocosm of an individual: each person changes dramatically throughout the course of their life, and yet maintains an integrity of identity. As such, there is the same imperative to protect culture as there is to protect the rights of each individual, once the concept of culture includes dissenting/ minority voices that form part of the wider culture's dialogues and internal diversities.

The case for the protection of the culture, and its dialogues, presented in this Chapter lays the foundation for the defence of the literary freedom as a cultural right – to be further outlined in Chapters 2 and 3 – as it posits both the importance of protecting culture (and cultural rights), and brings to the fore an often unacknowledged but highly relevant aspect of culture by foregrounding, following Butler's analysis, the centrality of transgressive and divergent voices. 'High art', such as literature, can be seen as one of the many voices that make up the everyday experience of culture, and one of the many voices which sustain the 'culture' to which people belong. It is 'culture' in this narrow sense (i.e. the Culture within culture, or, as it has traditionally been called, 'high art') that I will focus on in Chapter 2, in order to more fully outline the case for literary freedom as a cultural right.

Chapter 2

High Art, Elitism and Capabilities

The previous Chapter's analysis is one facet demonstrating that literary freedom of expression is a cultural right, and I will return to this in the examination of the social role of the writer in Chapter 3, bringing the arguments outlined in Chapter 1 and Chapter 2 together. Firstly, however, it is important to also address another prevailing question that arises in the academic debates on cultural rights – that is, should the state fund high art? Turning to this question again brings to the fore the problematic ambiguities in the word 'culture' in international legal mechanisms, which some legal theorists have noted place an implicit emphasis on the (undefined) concept of 'high culture', rather than "culture" in the anthropological sense, that, for instance, cultural anthropologist Pierre Bourdieu has analysed as the total system of everyday life.

The question of whether high art, or Culture deserves state support and funding is highly relevant to the question of what is entailed by freedom of (literary) expression, as if the case can be made that the state has a duty to support 'Culture' in the sense of high art such as literature, this in turn entails that freedom of literary expression is not merely a civil and political right that is to be protected by non-interference, but one which requires positive, proactive steps on behalf of states and other relevant actors. In other words, while in the pages above I outlined the (group-) right to 'culture' in the sense of 'the right to practice one's (everyday) culture', this Chapter argues for the right to 'Culture'.

With this in mind, I will here first outline Adorno's defence of preserving 'high culture' as a reserve against the 'culture industry' of popular art/ culture in capitalist societies, then present two arguments against Adorno's influential view: that it entails an elitism, and that it does not adequately explain why 'high culture' is exempt from Adorno's criticism of popular culture. I will then argue, however, that there is still a coherent case for promoting 'high art', which can be made by drawing upon the capabilities approach. Using the capabilities approach in this way has the further advantage of enabling us to unpick the traditional division of 'high art' and 'popular culture', which has until now been a problematic tension in the idea of culture both in academic discourse and international law.

2.1 The culture industry

Adorno and Horkheimer referred to twentieth century 'popular culture' (particularly television and popular music) as the "culture industry"[32] as they felt that 'popular culture' is a misnomer, given that, in their view, in advanced capitalist societies with mass-produced art, culture does not mirror society but shapes it – both commodifying values and creating a false sense of freedom in the general populace, which consolidates the power of the capitalist elite. Building upon Gramsci's reading of hegemony[33], Adorno linked popular culture to the Marxist idea of false-consciousness: through the commodification of culture, citizens are falsely taught to believe that they benefit from the capitalist system through the emancipatory element of 'choice' in consumerism and thus identify with capitalist society even though it runs counter to their own social/ economic interests and allegiance is bought at the expense of their actual freedom.

This process of creating a false sense of freedom (and thus inducing, in the general populace, passivity and compliance with capitalist inequalities) is, according to Adorno, performed in large part through the commodification of culture. In the culture industry, "the commercial character of culture causes the difference between culture and practical life to disappear."[34] Culture is thereby instrumentalised, as "reality becomes its own ideology through the spell cast by its faithful duplication. This is how the technological veil and the myth of the positive is woven."[35] This commodification of reality, through its duplication by the culture industry, leads, among other things, to a death of the imagination, that which conceives alternative modes of being. It thus reinforces the status quo, fulfilling only the false needs that the culture industry has taught people to want, rather than fulfilling their true human needs – which Adorno, following Marcuse[36], claims are: creativity, happiness and freedom.

Adorno's argument has since been reinforced by theorists such as Althusser, who argued that ideology is central to identity, that we build our identities around an ideology that "calls to us by name"[37] – in other words, that society makes the individual in its own image, and fosters the construction of identities that support the wider system of (namely, capitalist) society.

In contrast, the supposedly difficult high arts, which do not commodify values, provide a refuge against the duplication and distortion of reality by the popular "culture industry."

In this sense, high art plays an emancipatory role in society, satisfying people's true needs of creativity and freedom, as well as providing a mode of resistance to the total dominance of the "culture industry." Adorno's analysis is thus relevant to the question that frequently arises in discussion of cultural rights – whether the state should fund 'high' art that a numerically small number of people enjoy – because the "culture industry" concept demonstrates the weakness of a purely utilitarian argument about state funding.

In other words, whilst we may at face value argue that it is undemocratic, or unjust, to allocate government funds to forms of artistic expression that few people enjoy, Adorno's analysis of the instrumentalisation of popular culture presents a counter-argument: allowing the 'high arts' to thrive, and allowing all citizens of society to have access to these arts, would result in the greatest happiness of the greatest number, as those who appreciated high art would be truly happy, and truly free, whilst those who only engaged with "popular culture" would only have their 'false needs' met by the art/ culture they consumed.

2.2 Adorno's limitations

Yet although Adorno's analysis provides important insight into the power dynamics behind culture in a capitalist society, his thesis is open to several significant criticisms. The first is that Adorno's position – despite its grounding in Marxist theory – actually reinforces elitism; the second is that, even if popular culture reinforces capitalist power-structures, it does not necessarily follow that 'high art' is a remedy to this. I will briefly explore each of these arguments in turn. Firstly, it could be argued that Adorno's theory is in reality bound up primarily with a defence of the 'highbrow'– and at times self-consciously elitist – Modernist style, and, in presenting a dichotomy between popular art and (unpopular, difficult) Modernist art, Adorno reinforces the status quo even as he attempts to deconstruct it.

In addition, Adorno's thesis can be viewed through the lens of Berlin's distinction between the two kinds of 'liberty': the idea of 'false consciousness', or that people can be forced to be free by being *shown* what is in their true interests, is classically a position of positive liberty – those who subscribe to a more negative liberty viewpoint would thus counter Adorno's premise that, while people may think they are free, they are not free in objective reality.

If we take a negative liberty approach, we could argue that popular culture such as television programmes, would not be popular if it did not speak to people's desires and needs: if most people in a society choose television over opera or Modernist poetry, this simply means that their needs and desires are better met by television. Although this negative liberty argument can in turn be countered by Kymlicka's argument that people form their choices within culturally-defined contexts – and by the capabilities approach that is closely aligned with Kymlicka's argument, and which I will use to make the case for funding 'high art' – it is worth first noting that there are further drawbacks to Adorno's argument, even if we accept the idea that individual preferences are malleable.

Moreover, Adorno's critique is confined primarily to industrialised, capitalist society, which leaves a theoretical blind spot in his account of whether popular culture is instrumentalised by ideology in other kinds of societies. Perhaps the most notable example is many twentieth century Communist regimes, which overtly utilised and endorsed art forms such as socialist realism in order to reinforce the state's power by inculcating the state's ideology in the general populace. This can be seen, for instance, in the comment often attributed to Stalin, that writers are the "engineers of human souls"[38], and thus play a vital role in transmitting socialist ideals and values.

Of course, it does not logically follow that just because Adorno's argument is largely premised on a Marxist reading of freedom and ideology his theory is particularly undermined by the fact that twentieth-century Communist regimes, also grounded in Marxism, have used art to reinforce their ideological/ social power. The point remains, however, that Adorno's theory only attempts to account for the role of art in a specific kind of society, and thus is necessarily limited in its scope.

Perhaps a more significant criticism of Adorno is that other twentieth-century theorists – whilst broadly agreeing with Adorno's Marxist starting point on the construction of ideology – present contrasting accounts to Adorno's juxtaposition of the negative role of popular culture versus the emancipatory role of high art.

In particular, philosophers who see the construction of ideology as a discourse phenomenon generally agree that mass culture is is an ideological tool of capitalist society, but would disagree over whether 'high art' or Modernism is exempt from playing a role in the same process. Valentin Voloshinov, for instance, argued that "ideology is the struggle, at the level of signs, between antagonistic social interests"[39] and that all language or 'utterances' are necessarily utilised as means of control by the hegemonic elite.

Moreover, Habermas developed the idea of communicative action, which links Gramsci's theory of hegemony to language (or communication) itself. Habermas claims that ideology takes the form of distorted modes of communication, in which communication is subordinated to the reinforcement of existing power structures. In his explanation of the role of context, he goes on to claim that any communicative act can perform this role when reinforced by other communicative acts and located in a specific context, whereas Adorno's central argument rests upon the idea that 'high art' is not open to manipulations that would use it to reinforce ideology.

In other words, if we see the construction of ideology as a discourse phenomenon, and power dynamics as something built into language/ symbols/ communication itself, how is high art (which performs a 'communicative act' as much as Adorno's popular 'culture industry' does) any less part of the same process? Adorno does not seem to provide an adequate answer to this question, so even if his criticism of popular culture is valid, it does not in turn make the case for 'high art' as a tool of emancipation against ideology. While we do not need to agree with the Marxist analysis of those who see ideology as a discourse phenomenon, their insights are relevant here as they highlight the inconsistencies in Adorno's thesis.

2.3 Capabilities and high art

The capabilities approach can be utilised in this context to provide a more convincing case for why the state should fund 'high art'. As outlined in the Introduction, the capabilities approach presents significant advantages over other contemporary theories of political philosophy, in part because it acknowledges the role of "adaptive preferences" in shaping people's choices. This overlaps with Kymlicka's argument that an individual's choice is determined by the wider context. A capabilities reading of the question of funding 'high culture' would concur with Adorno's thesis that popular culture is more readily accessible – both by being more immediately comprehensible, and by being more physically accessible – to ordinary people than the traditional high arts such as opera. However, the fact that the majority of people in Western society prefer what could be framed either as popular or 'lowbrow' culture cannot simply be read (as negative liberty theorists might) as a neutral expression of their rational preference, nor, as Adorno reads it, as a sign of popular culture's inherent role as creator of damaging 'false needs.'

Instead, the lack of general public interest in the high arts can be seen as akin to the lack of women in the highest echelons of public life in societies where there are no legal overt obstacles to women holding positions of employment. Martha Nussbaum uses women as the key example of "adaptive preferences", claiming that women modify their goals and ambitions based on the cultural context, such as time-sanctioned ideas of a woman's role, and contemporary difficulties presented by women's integration into the workplace, which still often structurally functions in a gender-blind manner (or, in I. M. Young's terms, does not recognise and accommodate the different experience of women).

In other words, it does not require discriminatory legislation, or even overt sexism on the part of employers, to prevent women from achieving positions in the highest echelons of public/ cultural life: even when such overt obstacles are removed, if the cultural climate and gender-blind employment structure remain, women will continue to function with "adaptive preferences" of what is possible for them to achieve. The end result is the same as if there were overtly discriminatory legislation or sexist employment practices – i.e. a lack of women in the top positions.

This example has clear parallels with public participation/ interest in 'high art': like women in the workplace, the disadvantaged – or even simply the non-elite – within a society have adapted their preferences due to the time-sanctioned notion in (at least, Western) society, that 'high culture' is inaccessible, does not 'belong' to us, does not speak to or for us, and would not satisfy us. As with the example of women in the workplace, this creates two types of obligations on the part of the state: to change the formal and informal barriers to accessing 'high art', and to mitigate against 'adaptive preferences'. The first type entails firstly removing obstacles to 'high art', such as ensuring it is affordable (an obstacle removal that in practice likely entails the state funding of art), that it is available in different regions within the state and not only the cultural/ elite 'centre', and ensuring that 'high art' is available in languages of national minorities.

The second type of obligation on the part of states is more comprehensive, relating not to 'high culture' itself but to adaptive preferences as a whole: capabilities theory emphasises the inter-dependence of different economic, social and cultural rights in reality, as it is only when all core entitlements are secured that a person can meaningfully exercise a full range of choices, and thus pursue a fulfilled life.

Mitigating against the 'adaptive preferences' that make most people feel they cannot appreciate 'high art' thus entails numerous obligations on the state in all aspects of a person's life, such as literacy, education, bodily integrity, and so on. It is only when the full range of entitlements are secured, and, on the other side, 'high art' made meaningfully accessible, that people would be a position to choose, without mitigating circumstances, whether or not they prefer 'high art' or 'popular culture.'

It is worth noting that, under this approach, high art is not invested with the same normative value as Adorno's schema seems to imply: if, once people have secured a full range of entitlements, and can exercise their full human capability, they choose not to, for instance, attend the opera or read Modernist poetry, this has no innate significance under the capabilities approach, and no longer indicates a societal inequality.

Similarly, if – after women as a group were no longer subject to 'adaptive preferences' on their concept of their own potential – women generally chose not to compete for high positions in public life, this would no longer be an indictment of the society's gender inequality. Enjoying 'high art' or 'Culture', or holding a high public office, is not imbued with intrinsic value – securing the full range of entitlements is necessary merely to ensure people can fully exercise their choice on whether or not to pursue these goals or interests. However, it should be borne in mind that in both the case of women's employment and the case of the general public's access to high culture, comprehensive measures and changes in societal attitudes need to take place before we can reasonably suggest that their absence from high public roles/ lack of interest in 'high art' is merely a sign of fully emancipated, empowered people 'expressing their personal preferences'.

Applying the capabilities approach in this way also has the further advantage of helping us to unpack the problematic ambiguities latent in the different concepts of 'culture', and what constitutes 'high culture'. In capitalistic and class-based societies in particular, the very definition of high art is predicated upon the idea that it is difficult art that only the 'highly educated' (and thus 'highly cultured', in the traditional sense) can appreciate. Many nineteenth- and twentieth century defences of 'high art' entailed a defence of the socio-economic – and, above all, cultural – elite as a distinct strata of society. Modernist poet T.S. Eliot argued that poets, in particular, were patrician figures in society akin to Platonic philosopher-rulers, whose duty was to "purify the dialect of the tribe", and as such were required to create difficult, coded art that only the educated 'elite' could be expected to understand.[40]

Similarly, while influential Victorian critic Matthew Arnold argued that great art should "do away with classes", his defence of 'high art' was largely predicated on the idea that the capitalist middle-classes/ bourgeoisie of the industrial revolution were inevitably "Philistines" (in the Orientalist, Victorian sense of 'uncultured'), who would never transcend their class-destiny and fully appreciate 'true' art. In other words, the traditional defence in favour of keeping – and funding – unpopular or difficult art forms has simultaneously required a defence of elitism. If the capabilities approach were fully applied to art, as outlined above, it would no longer be 'high art' in the sense that it would be bound up with an elitist worldview, or art that was out of the reach of the general populace, either through being too expensive or because factors such as literary, education, and time-consuming work prevented the majority from being able to enjoy it. In this sense, the capabilities approach both provides a case for supporting 'high art' in society and, simultaneously, removes the need for the concept of 'high art' itself.

In conclusion, there is a valid argument that there is an imperative on the part of the state to fund 'high art', such as literature, even if this art is not consumed by the majority of people. Adorno has made the case for the importance of high culture's emancipatory role against the ideological instrumentalisation of the "culture industry." However, as shown above, his argument is, in turn, subject to several criticisms, notably the negative liberty reading of freedom, the risk that Adorno may be reinforcing elitism, and the criticism of those who see ideology as a discourse phenomenon, who could argue that high art has the potential to play the same function as the popular "culture industry" in reinforcing power structures.

Subsequently, the position for the imperative of funding and otherwise supporting high art should instead be made through a reading of capabilities theory, which entails that the state fund art of all forms, and simultaneously provide comprehensive provision of economic, social and cultural rights – notably education – so that the disadvantaged in society are not shaped by their circumstances to find 'high art' inaccessible. In turn, providing each individual with the full entitlement to their capabilities would entail that the concept of 'high art' itself changes, as no art form or artistic style would be inaccessible to the disadvantaged –a reality on which the concept of 'high art' has traditionally been predicated.

Chapter 3

The Writer in Society

This Chapter brings together the lines of analysis of the two previous Chapters – culture as a group right; the importance of art (in this case, the importance of literature) – with the emphasis in the traditional/ negative liberty understanding of freedom of expression, which is concerned primarily with the rights of the individual writer. It is necessary to now bring all these strands together, as the dynamics between the two – the individual writer, and the culture/ society as a whole – bring to the fore the crux of the interdependency between first and second generation rights: the (civil and political) rights of the individual writer, and the (economic, social and cultural) rights of the community at large.

In the following paragraphs, I will first outline the concept of the writer as a social being (and the consequent issue of self-censorship), then look at the relationship in reverse: the impact that writers have on societies. Then, returning to the international legal mechanisms relevant to literary freedom as a cultural right, this Chapter will point to the kinds of positive steps states should take in order to ensure both access to culture (i.e., in this case, literature) and the freedom of the writer.

The relationship between the two is essentially symbiotic: writers arise out of, and to some extent speak on behalf of, the society at large – and yet academics writing on the subject of 'world literature' assert that literature also belongs to humanity as a whole; conversely, societies or 'cultures' need individual creators of art (in this case, writers) to shape, reinforce, preserve and exercise the identity of the group.

Moreover, we cannot take the balance (or 'justness') of this relationship for granted: positive state action is required to ensure the dynamics protect both group rights and the rights of the writer. As this Chapter will outline, ensuring justice in the dynamics of the writer-society relationship entails that we must uphold both civil and political and, simultaneously, economic, social and – above all – cultural rights.

3.1 The 'Death of the Author' versus the 'moral imagination'

Roland Barthes's influential essay 'The Death of the Author'[41] posited that, from the reader's perspective, the author of a text is now dead; the text stands alone outside of the author's intent, and that now, once "the author is removed, the claim to decipher a text becomes quite futile", the text is instead a tissue of quotations drawn from "innumerable centres of culture"[42] continually rewriting itself through the eyes of the reader, and what the reader brings to it.

In Barthes's understanding, this is not just a conceptual shift but a temporal phenomenon, occurring at the moment of (or, as Barthes's causality is unclear, *defining* the moment of) modernity: prior to this epochal shift, the author was considered to "nourish the book, which is to say he exists before it, thinks, suffers, lives for it, is in the same relation of antecedence to his work as a father to his child."[43] In contrast to this, the text in modernity is removed from the author: "the modern scriptor is born simultaneously with the text; is in no way equipped with a being preceding or exceeding the writing, is not the subject with the book as predicate; there is no other time than that of the enunciation and every text is eternally written here and now."[44]

Barthes's influential viewpoint, which is the foundations of postmodernist literary theory and critical theory, is highly relevant to the task at hand here, of examining the social role of the writer, and the relationship between the writer and society. After all, if we take on board Barthes's position, does this mean that we cannot talk about the writer as a social being, or – as will be explored in Chapter 4 – the responsibility of the author (such as the author Radovan Karadžić, with his overtly ultranationalist poetry) towards the society?

At first glance, it feels as though a refutation of Barthes's viewpoint would necessarily entail taking up a disappointingly reactionary position in opposition: that is, to reiterate some kind of Victorian conception of the author's responsibility and the finality of one single, 'authoritative' interpretation of a literary text. I hope to show here, however, that there are ways to interrogate Barthes's position, and reassert the idea of the social role of the writer, without falling into this reactionary pitfall: the first is Trilling's alternative reading of the shift in modernity towards the text, and the second is through a delineation of the idea of the 'writer' as opposed to the 'author', which leaves much of Barthes's thesis intact whilst also allowing room for the idea of the "moral imagination." One initial criticism that could be levelled at Barthes is his reading of the temporal shift towards the *authorless* text.

This has generally been accepted by later theorists, but Lionel Trilling, for instance, in his study of sincerity and authenticity in modern literature, charts a shift in entirely the opposite direction: one towards valuing the literary 'text' for its sincerity of voice, situated in an understanding of the 'authenticity' of the writer who produced it. He notes this shift in post-1945 Western literature, as well as how it has come to change the way in which earlier works of Western literature are read, for instance: "we are no longer required to regard as wholly fortuitous the fact that the hero of [Marcel] Proust's novel is named Marcel, [and] within the last two decades English and American poets have programmatically scuttled the sacred doctrine of the persona, the belief that the poet does not, must not, present himself to us and figure in our consciousness as a person, as a man speaking to men, but must have an exclusively aesthetic experience."[45]

This shift towards the recognition of the writer in the work mirrors the broader cultural shift in Western sensibility towards the recognition of, or conceptual development of, the 'self', which Trilling places as occurring with the Enlightenment: before this occurred, man did "not have an awareness of what one historian, Georges Gusdorf, calls *internal space*", upon which the value of 'authenticity', of being true to oneself, is predicated. Since the Enlightenment, however, authenticity of the 'voice' of the writer has, according to Trilling's analysis, come to be of supreme importance in the way in which Western literature is read (mirroring sociologist Richard Sennett's analysis, in *The Fall of Public Man*, that in twentieth-century late-capitalist societies, the "ideology of intimacy" came to supercede the value of correctly and self-consciously performing one's public 'role'.[46])

We could therefore query Barthes's assertion that the authorless text has superceded the experience of the authored text. Nonetheless, Trilling's alternative reading of the temporal shift towards the author-in-the-work, or authenticity rather than 'authorlessness', perhaps does not get to the heart of the distinction between Barthes's idea and the idea of the writer as a social being, which is the focus of this Chapter. To further make this case, and assert the validity of the 'writer as a social being' despite Barthes's position, it is worth making the distinction between the *author* and the *writer*.

In other words, Barthes's analysis of how texts perform 'without an author' may be valid, but it pertains only to the role of the author –however, this does not render illegitimate attempts by social historians, sociologists, and so on, to talk about the specific individuals who produce these texts, the writers, and the relation of these individuals to those around them. Barthes is not concerned with the 'writer', and does not intend to undertake an analysis of the writer's role in society; in short, he is addressing a different question.

As Susan Swann has argued: the author may be dead after Barthes, but the writer, and the writer's conscience, is real. Swann goes on to argue that the concept of the imagination, a central tool of any literary writer, is closely linked to the concept of a conscience, and that these synthesise into a kind of "moral imagination."[47] Swann argues that this in no way entails that good writers ought to create 'moralistic', didactic art, but simply an acknowledgement that writers work within societies, and inevitably absorb and reflect their moral codes. She states that the "author may be dead, but the writer lives...and she possesses important human attributes that go hand in hand with the act of making literature, an imagination and a conscience...which is expressed in unique ways in public life...the literary imagination is the writer's conscience in action."[48] Despite Barthes' concept of the authorless text, and the detached author, the writer as an inevitably social being can be seen as akin to any other individual in Kymlicka's analysis, as a moral agent who makes choices within a culturally-prescribed context: the "moral imagination" of the author arises out of the cultural context inhabited by the writer as an individual.

While it is beyond the remit of my work here to fully explore the cultural history of the social role of the writer, it is worth briefly reiterating the role of the writer particularly in the construction of European nationalisms: Hobsbawm and Ranger, for instance, have shown the central role of Romanticism in the primordialist understanding of nationhood, particularly through the celebration, 'reclamation' (and, in cases such as the invented Scottish poet Ossian, fabrication) of ancient 'national' poetry and music, as part of the invented traditions of nascent nationalisms.

Moreover, in his essay 'The Role of the Writer in a New Nation' the writer Chinua Achebe also notes the link between literature and the nation.[49] Whilst dismissing 'nationalist art', Achebe argues that to deny that a writer, particularly a non-Western writer, is a social being who speaks on behalf of their 'group' or culture, is to reinforce the false neutrality of the white/Western (and, it could be added, straight) male literary canon, which falsely claims to speak on behalf of the human condition as a whole, rather than recognising its cultural biases and privileges. To rephrase Achebe's argument in I. M. Young's terms: to insist that the author's experience (including cultural experience) has no bearing on the text entails a denial of difference that reinforces existing power structures.

3.2 The impact of society on the writer; the impact of the writer on society

If writers are social beings who arise out of their cultural context, it follows that this context has a bearing not only how their work is received or 'read' by their culture, but also has an effect on the writer *as* s/he is writing. Perhaps the most obvious impact that society, or the cultural climate, has on the individual writer is that of self-censorship. In his essay 'The Freedom of the Press', George Orwell commented, in reference to British literature during the Second World War, that official censorship had been insignificant; instead "the sinister fact about literary censorship in England is that it is largely voluntary."[50] Orwell argues that self-censorship occurs when writers fear not official sanctioning but widespread disapproval from 'their audience' (which, for the purposes of this argument, can be broadly read as 'the wider society in which they reside'); in order to maintain their place in society – or their place as a member of the literary establishment/ intelligensia – a writer chooses not to present unpopular views, or unpopular/ unfashionable styles, in their public work.

If we see cultural groups or societies as wholly homogenous, it could be argued that self-censorship by individual writers is no loss to the society, as the writer only self-censors only that which s/he knows the culture would not want. However, it is important to restate the earlier point, in the face of this argument, that transgressive voices are an integral part of culture, and that culture – and cultural rights – cannot be meaningfully exercised if culture/ society is treated as a static, ahistorical and homogenous entity without its own internal pluralities of voices.

In other words, while some self-censorship is inevitable (because writers, as rational self-interested beings, are likely to respond to the desires of their audience, and tailor their output to the literary 'market') it is imperative to mitigate against the self-censorship of dissenting voices, as this harms not only the individual writer (who is forced not to express her/ himself), but also the cultural group, who loses out on one of the plurality of voices that *make up* their culture, regardless of the argument frequently deployed by traditionalists *within* a society – such as those who condemned Rushdie for publishing *The Satanic Verses* – that dissenting voices are "not a part of their culture."

The importance of protecting against self-censorship brings to the fore the other side of the coin in the writer-society dynamic: the society's need for individual creators of art, art which then informs the identity of the group as a whole. While it could be seen as ethnocentric to argue that societies need *writers*, as this argument privileges cultures which have a tradition of writing, there is the anthropological argument that all societies/ groups have roles of story-tellers in order to preserve the shared heritage of the group. In societies that do have a written tradition, writers and poets have often played this role: an early example often cited is the role of the psychological novel *The Tale of Genji* in early medieval Japan. Moreover, the impact of European colonialism on many societies/ nations worldwide intersected with existing practices of storytelling, creating new modes of artistic expression; decolonisation did not necessarily entail rejection of 'European' artistic influences on post-colonial artists/ writers.

As Terry Eagleton has detailed at length, subversive literature from the writers from the colonial periphery often "uses the canon against itself" – Rushdie's reworking of early Islamic history in a post-modernist vision, and Joyce's use of the myth of Ulysses (when the Greek/ Roman 'Classics' were seen to belong to the Anglo colonial/ civilisational 'centre') both signal the transgressive, and emancipatory, potential of literature itself, which reworks the Orientalist, hierarchical canon of Western literature to articulate the experiences of those who have been silenced or marginalised by the colonial experience.

Still, there is no denying that, throughout history, written literature has been the preserve of specific cultures, and the domain only of the elite within those cultures: it is worth reminding ourselves that, even today, it is an art form that excludes much of humanity. So can it be argued that "societies need writers?" Perhaps a more helpful argument is that, in societies with a tradition of written literature, any move to oppress writers, or suppress literature, harms the society as a whole.

Cultural historians examining the impact of the post-1968 authoritarianism on Czechoslovakian society have noted the impact that the purges of the 400 writers had on the society's sense of identity: Culik notes that the impact on the nation's psyche extended far beyond the urban/ educated/ elite intelligensia who had previously been actively engaged in the heart of literary culture; people at all levels of society felt that their culture had 'lost its voice.'[51]

Culik and others have noted the centrality of cultural concept of the 'emigre writer' to post-1968 Czechoslovakian identity, and that the dominant cultural figure of the writer-in-exile, most notably embodied in writers such as Kundera and Havel, reformulated the whole basis of Czechoslovakian (and Czech and Slovak) identity. In other words, even a brief examination of what occurs when a society loses its greatest and most popular writers indicates that it is an injustice not just to the individual writers, but to the society as a whole.

3.3 The writer-society relationship

The figure of the writer in exile brings to the fore the symbiotic relationship between the individual writer and society/ societies. The novelist and poet Wole Soyinka, commenting on his own condition of exile, noted that, while many writers insist on "an exile persona that feeds on the community of the alienated" – and that celebrates the transgression of boundaries, such as national boundaries – a writer's exile also brings with it "the weight of a distant cultural longing",[52] as the writer as an individual is inevitably *from* one society, one culture or group, in particular. Theorists who address the concept of 'world literature' also note that literature occupies a peculiar position of both belonging to a particular group, and belonging to humanity as a whole.

David Damrosch has shown how literary works "manifest differently abroad than at home", but still nonetheless belong to a "global dialogue"[53], while Pascale Casanova notes that all writers 'inherit' the traditions of the literary culture from which they emerge, and can only choose what to do in the face of this: "national literary and linguistic patrimony supplies a sort of a priori definition of the writer, one that he will transform (if need be, by rejecting it or, as in the case of [Samuel] Beckett, by conceiving himself in opposition to it) throughout his career."[54] In short, the role of the writer within society echoes and articulates the complexity of the the individual, especially the 'transgressive' or 'subversive' individual, within the culture that formed them and to which they belong.

Understanding the relationship between the writer and society is a key component of the argument that literary freedom is a cultural right, and clarifies the kinds of positive steps that states should take in order to ensure both access to culture (in this case, literature) and the freedom of the writer. As Chapter 2 made the case for the state funding of the arts and the capabilities approach's defence of 'high art', the interrelated needs of the writer and society outlined in this Chapter indicate that state policies regarding literary freedom, must ensure that both 'sides' can fulfil their role in the relationship. Several concrete – although far from comprehensive – suggestions for how to navigate this relationship emerge from the analysis of the writer and society:

Firstly, it entails, most obviously, the negative liberty position that writers must not have their civil and political right to freedom of expression arbitrarily encroached upon by the state, although the gravity of this individual right (which could be seen as an 'Article 19 of the UDHR' right) is now strengthened by the insight that the society also suffers, as in Czechoslovakia, when the civil and political rights of writers are violated.

Secondly, it entails that state policy on the arts in some sense protects the writer from the society, in the sense of societal pressure – as Orwell noted, self-censorship is the detrimental effect of 'society' on the individual writer's freedom; and the symbiotic relationship sketched above shows that this, in turn, negatively affects society as a whole, by denying (as established by Butler's analysis) their right to the full plurality of the voices within their own culture. In other words, self-censorship is not simply an 'Article 19 of the UDHR' issue, but also an 'Article 27 of ICCPR and Article 15 of ICESCR' issue, as self-censorship by writers entails the society cannot fully "participate in culture." Measures against self-censorship could perhaps include active state sponsorship or state encouragement of a variety of transgressive and challenging literary voices, including the voices of 'minorities within minorities', through funding, prizes, state broadcasting, and so on.

It is interesting to note that in Britain, the anti-censorship arts organisation Index on Arts (a sub-chapter of Index on Censorship) has devoted detailed reports and events solely to the issue of artistic *self*-censorship. It could well be argued that governments have a duty to respond to, or even commission (if there is no Index on Arts-type organisation in civil society) reports into artistic self-censorship in their state, and otherwise take steps to mitigate against this factor in public life.

Thirdly, it should be noted briefly here, that the counter-balancing duty to the self-censorship issue (of 'protecting the right from society') would presumably be 'protecting society from the writer': namely, protecting society, particularly margi-nalised groups, from literary hate speech, such as the ultranatio-nalist poetry produced by Radovan Karadžić. The issue of literary hate speech, and when it is permissible to for the state censor on these grounds, has traditionally been seen as a violation of civil and political rights. Chapter 4 will outline how this issue can also be addressed through the capabilities approach, so that the desire to uphold the principle of 'freedom of expression', and the duty to mitigate against the harm that hate speech causes to those targetted by it, are no longer proble-matically juxtaposed, and we can move beyond the language of 'striking a balance' between these two concerns, making them instead mutually-reinforcing.[55]

Fourthly, the insights brought from Wole Soyinka's description of the state of the "writer in exile", and analysis by Damrosch and others on the complexities latent in the concept of "world literature", indicate perhaps the most central imperative in state funding of literature, and in the arts in general. That is, given that the writer both speaks on behalf of, and emerges from a particular 'group' and nation, yet is simultaneously engaged in cross-cultural (and, Damrosch argues, even multi-temporal[56]) dialogue, the state *must not*, through its funding of arts, force the writers it subsidises or otherwise supports into the position of being a 'national', or nationalist, 'voice of the people'. To place conditions on state funding of literature that writers must exalt, and 'speak for', the nation alone, would both deny the crucial transgressive element of culture, and limit the writer's capacity to engage in the cross-cultural/ cross-temporal dialogue of world literature.

As the relationship between writer and society is mutually-dependent, depriving writers of the change to participate in this world literature 'dialogue' in turn diminishes the audience/ society's capability to participate in cultural life. This is equally true of conditional state support of the arts that forces the writer to exalt, not the 'nation', but the state's ideology or dogma in other aspects: Stalin's conception of writers as "engineers of human souls" to be utilised to inculcate the masses with Communist ideology, for instance, similarly deprives the writer – and consequently the society, and the writer's various audiences – of their ability to fully participate in the broader 'dialogue' of literature.

Fifthly, the insights brought from the application of the capabilities approach to access to literature/ the arts (as outlined in Chapter 2) can be added to these recommendations, and relate primarily to the 'society' side of the writer-society relationship: that the right to fully participate in cultural life entails, in turn, a comprehensive variety of positive state actions. These actions do not relate to 'high culture', or the funding of and protection of the arts itself, but to ensuring all of the necessary 'entitlements' that would allow individuals to fully enjoy culture, rather than being limited by their 'adaptive preferences.'

This includes a sweepingly broad range of entitlements, such as literacy, education, health provision, and gender parity. Whilst this is the broadest and most challenging recommendation, with impacts far beyond the sphere of 'access to the arts', it is still illuminating to further underscore the parallels between role the writer and the society: read another way, the detrimental effect of 'adaptive preferences' could be seen as the 'self-censorship' of large portions of society, inasmuch as, according to Nussbaum, disadvantaged groups such as ethnic minorities, women, and the disabled, are not, in liberal democracies, explicitly forbidden from fully exercising their human entitlements – just as, in Orwell's conception of self-censorship, the writer is not explicitly forbidden from publishing – but, in both cases, the broader social, economic and cultural conditions shape their choices, and to this extent limit their fulfilment.

To summarise, this Chapter has attempted to outline the mutually-dependent and symbiotic relationship between the individual writer and the society at large, in order both to demonstrate the mutual dependence of first and second generation rights, and to enable us to highlight five key imperatives of state funding of the arts in keeping with the capabilities approach. The artist, or writer, emerges from, in some sense 'speaks for', and needs society, just as societies need artists (and thus, in many cultural contexts worldwide, writers) – thus the state has a duty to fully enable all aspects of this relationship.

Chapter 4

Literary Hate Speech – Solutions Beyond Censorship

Let us return now to the event in April 2009, when PEN Slovakia, an organisation which campaigns on behalf of persecuted writers and in favour of free expression[57], issued a statement condemning the publication in a Slovakian journal of a poem by Radovan Karadžić. For one important remaining facet of any understanding of literary freedom is the concept of the limits, which are framed in terms of 'hate speech'.[58] In other words, addressing the question of whether PEN Slovakia's condemnation of the publication of Karadžić's poetry contradicts its self-declared standpoint on freedom of literary expression, is a lens through which to demonstrate the inadequacies of the traditional approach to freedom of expression, and how the capabilities approach – which Katherine Gelber has applied to hate speech – provides a more effective remedy to this ongoing dilemma.

Turning now to literary hate speech is intended to complete the last main aspect of the argument that has been advanced throughout my overall argument here. As I made the case for the 'social role of the writer' and the dynamics of aspects of the writer-society relationship in Chapter 3, it was noted that the flipside to the necessity of 'protecting the writer from society' (that is, protecting the writer from both censorship and the kind of *self*-censorship outlined by Orwell) would be 'protecting society from the writer', in instances where a writer's works could cause tangible damage to disadvantaged groups – namely, through literary hate speech.

Again, as first stated in the Introduction, the term literary hate speech applies only to literature which causes tangible harm, such as incitement to racial hatred or – as could be argued in the case of Karadžić's poetry – incitement to genocide, not to literary works which cause offence to cultural groups, even if these cultural groups are minorities in a disadvantaged position vis-à-vis the wider society or nation state.

The topic of hate speech and art is fundamentally linked to central issues of political philosophy, namely the issue of liberty and at what point it is justifiable to intervene in someone's liberty to protect others. Considering the issue of hate speech in atypical cases like literature provides a way to explore this broader issue of hate speech as a whole, although the focus here will be particularly on literary (and artistic) hate speech, in keeping with my aim to apply capabilities theory to literary freedom, and assert that literary freedom is a cultural as well as civil and political right. Here I will focus the study on moral, rather than legal, definitions of hate speech.[59]

Hate speech can be defined as speech (or symbolic speech, such as non-language-based symbols) which paints a derogatory picture of others on grounds of race, gender, ethnicity, sexual orientation, etc., which incites aggression against that group. For the purpose of this analysis, it works to provisionally accept that all hate speech has the potential to incite harmful social movements and social violence, as it is widely accepted that most hate speech performs this act, and the theoretical example of 'hate speech which fails to incite' is of less immediate concern.[60]

Both PEN Slovakia and the journal which published his poetry over-simplified the dilemma of whether we censor hate speech in artistic works. Given the failure of the traditional debate on free speech, we must build a position on hate speech that centres around two ideas: the importance of context and the necessity to provide a forum for those affected by hate speech to 'speak back'. Demonstrating the applicability of the capabilities approach to this issue, this Chapter intends to assert that only a 'positive liberty' approach can provide a position in which the principle of upholding freedom of speech and the 'goal' of diminishing the harmful effects of hate speech can be complementary and mutually-reinforcing.

4.1 Karadžić and poetic ultranationalism

It is firstly important to outline the issue of Karadžić's poetry, in order to situate it in the broader context of hate speech. I believe that Karadžić's poetry does constitute 'hate speech', although such a belief does not necessarily entail the conclusion that we must therefore censor it. Karadžić's poetry requires explanation because it is highly atypical of 'hate speech', and one problem with the traditional debate on freedom of expression – outlined in the Introduction – is that is does not accommodate this kind of hate speech, focused as it is on explicit communication rather than subtle and allegorical modalities of hate speech. I will first consider Karadžić's 'poet-warrior' identity, secondly the content of the poetry, and thirdly the manner in which Karadžić's poetry is linked to his actions and commands in 1992-1995.

Karadžić was once known primarily as a poet and poetry is also central to his self-identity. Surdukowski notes that a "self-romanticizing macho" aesthetic runs through poems in which Karadžić writes in the first-person voice of a 'poet.'[61] More generally, in both his poetry and statements about poetry, Karadžić repeated the theme of poet-warrior identity, in which the creative act of poetry is inextricably bound up with the poet's role as a soldier, an identity which is mirrored in the frequent military motifs and poetry in which war is the subject matter.[62] Although we cannot conclude from this that his poetry constitutes hate speech, it is worth acknowledging: Karadžić himself sees his poetry and his activity as a 'warrior' as conceptually inseparable.

It is also worth highlighting the fact that Karadžić's poetry has sold widely and won numerous awards: for instance, in 1994 the Russian Writer's Union awarded Karadžić the Mikhail Sholokov Prize, their highest prize for poetry. New collections of his poetry were even published after the ICTY warrant for his arrest was issued. While it does not logically follow that the popularity and occasional literary 'acclaim' of his poetry has a bearing on whether or not the poetry itself can be deemed to constitute hate speech, it is worth bearing in mind the practical issue of such popularity: namely, that if his poetry constitutes hate speech, Karadžić had and still has a wide forum and readership to whom he can disseminate his poetic 'message' of incitement to social violence.

Moreover, if we attempt to approach Karadžić's poetry 'blind' (i.e. not knowing who wrote it) it is impossible not to be struck by the predominance of imagery relating to militarised and ritualised violence, purity, 'cleansing' and ethnic superiority.

His poetry could be divided into two categories: firstly, those which reconstruct and re-appropriate ancient history, particularly in frequent allusion to the 1389 Battle of Kosovo; secondly, poems in a contemporary setting, which simultaneously fetishise modern warfare and mourn the lost Eden of ancient Serbia. These two strands come together in Karadžić's poet-warrior identity, which allows him to stitch himself neatly into a mythologised present day, in which Karadžić re-enacts the role of an ancient hero in a war which is both modern and of 'mythic' proportions.

The central problem Karadžić's poetry presents to us, however, is the issue of 'explicitness'. Andrew Rubin has described Karadžić's poetry as "a psychic landscape of eerie and illogical violence"[63], but although war is a central theme (in poems such as 'War Boots', and 'Grenade') it is often metaphorical, either using military metaphors to describe natural scenes, like hurling a grenade at the "ambush of dawn"[64] or using lyrical, 'natural' language to describe war scenes. This presents immediate problems for discerning 'hate speech', which we normally consider to be explicit and uncoded. Moreover, allegories and metaphors abound, such as depictions of Sarajevo as a 'bride' waiting for the 'poet-warrior'.

At face value, it would be hard to read such symbolic, non-literal language as incitement to violence. However, when taken together with his reconstruction/ reappropriation of ancient history, this fetishisation of violence and purity combines to form a comprehensive 'code' which expresses an entire worldview: a worldview of Serbian ultranationalism, in which violence against others is obligated by the 'pure'. If we locate Karadžić's work within the landscape of other Serbian-nationalist artists and their audience, it is clear that Karadžić's code is not a private one, but one which his intended audience would have understood, and which Karadžić knew his audience would understand.

4.2 Cultural climate

Although it is beyond the remit of my exploration here to provide a comprehensive social history of Serbian ultranationalism and its key figures, it is worth briefly noting the role that writers and artists could be said to have played in stoking ultranationalism during the period Milošević was in power, as locating Karadžić's poetry in the broader artistic climate better illuminates how his poetry could perform the 'act' of incitement to social violence. Although it would be overstating the case to say that writers played a larger role in Serbian ultranationalism than they have in other exclusivist ideologies or regimes, Rei Shigeno has shown how Serbian-nationalist intellectuals, particularly writers, were central to rehabilitating the concept of exclusivist nationalism during the 1980s by deftly articulating it within the rubric of socialism, so that it could no longer be dismissed as a bourgeois idea.

Shigeno shows how the Serbian writer (and later President) Dobrica Cosic was the first figure to raise the issue of nationalism some twenty years before. By the 1980s, when the discourse on nationalism had shifted significantly, Cosic became a crucial signatory of the Memorandum by the Serbian Academy of Arts and Sciences, which was later used as evidence at the ICTY, as it provided evidence of 'rationale' or *mens rea* for crimes committed during the 1990s. Nor was artistic construction of nationalism only enacted by writers or other traditionally 'highbrow' artists: Robert Hudson has written on the role popular music played in the construction of Serbian exclusivist identity in the 1980s and 1990s.[65] Situating Karadžić's poetry in this broader artistic landscape gives us a clearer idea of its potential to communicate an ultranationalist agenda: even if (and it is likely that) his poetry alone would not have been enough to construct an ultranationalist climate, when taken together with other persuasive and popular constructions of nationalism in art, its 'code' gained both a veneer of legitimacy and an artistic potency through which it could efficiently disseminate a message of exclusivism and sectarianism.

A related issue is the way in which Karadžić used his poetry during his time as a military leader. Surdukowski notes that, throughout the conflict, Karadžić would recite both his own poetry and the poetry of nineteenth-century nationalist poets like Njegos during his visits to the frontline.[66] Moreover, documentary footage by Paul Pawlikowski provides evidence of Karadžić and Russian ultranationalist Limonov reciting poetry and simultaneously firing down on to Sarajevo, literally linking their involvement in war crimes and their poetic 'activity' in the same moment in time. In a gruesome sense, then, it could be said that Karadžić perhaps provides a paradigm of the circle of hate speech: as seen in Pawlikowski's footage, he himself performs the act that his works incited others to perform.

In other words, if we take hate speech to be speech that incites social violence, there can be little doubt that Karadžić's poetry fulfils this criteria. Having established this, in one sense the question is just: what should we *do* about Karadžić's hate speech? Before we address this, however, we must note two problems: firstly, the issue of 'explicitness', secondly, the dilemma of whether the fact that Karadžić-as-an-individual committed war crimes weighs upon on how we treat Karadžić's poetry. While Karadžić's unique role as both propagator of artistic hate speech and enactor of war crimes provides a way of conceptually capturing the whole 'cycle' of hate speech, it is not clear that this overrides the basic principle that we must always separate the biography of an artist from analysis of the artwork itself.

This issue — of what to do when one individual is, for instance, both-Riefenstahl-and-Hitler-simultaneously, that is, both creator of artistic hate speech and a central political figure in a genocidal or fascistic regime – is perhaps not such of a practical concern here if we consider that, as this Chapter has shown, Karadžić's poetry constitutes hate speech even if we read it 'blind'. It does, however, raise the theoretical question of what to do about art by perpetrators of social violence, war crimes and genocide, when the art produced by such individuals does *not* constitute hate speech, but does lend that figure some veneer of legitimacy or sympathy with their 'audience'. Such questions are, however, largely beyond the scope of my exploration here.

To reiterate, even a cursory study of the broader cultural climate in which Karadžić 's poetry was operating demonstrates that its coded, metaphorical allusions and implications would have been understood by the intended audience, who could situate them in the broader ultranationalist discourse, and thus fully grasp the darker implications relating to, amongst other messages, the dehumanisation of Bosnian Muslims, and the 'rightness' of actions that further dehumanised, or, in Karadžić 's cruelly euphemistic language, 'cleansed' Bosnian Muslims. How such 'coded' literary hate speech, which implicitly incites genocidal activities, should be dealt with, is the subject of the following pages.

Before this, however, it is worth briefly noting that in dealing with Karadžić's poetry, we are dealing with hate speech of a specific type – that is, genocidal hate speech. This is worth pointing out in order to distinguish this discussion from, for instance, misogynist or sexist hate speech which, while highly damaging, do not fit the 1948 Convention on Genocide's criteria of incitement to "destroy, in whole or in part, a national, ethnical, racial or religious group."

Although the *indirectness* of Karadžić's poetry, as outlined above, leaves open the question of whether it fulfils the criteria of *"direct* and public incitement" in the Convention on Genocide, the point remains that his poetry does not constitute mere hate speech, but genocidal hate speech, however covert. Although it is beyond the remit of my analysis here to explore this in more detail, it is also worth noting here that the uniqueness of genocide, and thus the uniqueness of genocidal hate speech as opposed to other forms of hate speech, brings to the fore tension between – on the one hand – the need for the 'individualisation of guilt' as emphasised in transitional justice theory and the legal framework of war crimes tribunals – and, on the other hand, the emphasis in social science analysis of genocide, of the broader 'cultural climate' that enabled genocide to be enacted, which has been explored by theorists such as Arendt, Adorno and Zygmunt Bauman. The following sub-chapters will explore further cases of what could be deemed 'genocidal hate speech', before pointing to the ways in which this can be addressed more adequately than the traditional 'freedom of expression' debate has been able to.

4.3 Art and fascism

In her influential essay 'Fascinating Fascism', Susan Sontag criticises the resuscitation of the reputation of Nazi filmmaker Leni Riefenstahl, and in doing so presents two key aspects missing from the traditional freedom of expression debate. The first is the overlap of fascistic art and 'legitimate' Western culture, which highlights the traditional debate's failure both to address the idea of the 'grey line' between hate speech and non-hate speech and its failure to focus on the issue of 'genocidal' hate speech in particular; the second is the importance of context, which takes us part-way towards a solution. This sub-chapter will consider each of Sontag's insights in turn.

Firstly, in analysing the work of Nazi filmmaker Riefenstahl, Sontag outlines the 'bleed' of fascistic art into culture we deem legitimate. Sontag links the renewed celebration of Riefenstahl's work in the 1970s to the latent, undetected continuation of Nazi aesthetics in Western art.[67] She argues that Riefenstahl's reputation was 'de-Nazified' because the presence of these themes in her work were mistakenly taken to indicate that she was not involved in the project of constructing a Nazi aesthetic and providing a kind of visual reinforcement of Nazi values; Sontag, however, argues that this is because fascist aesthetic is entirely consistent with broader trends of Western art, including supposedly progressive art in the 1970s. She writes: "it is generally thought that National Socialism stands only for brutishness and terror. But this is not true. National Socialism – more broadly, fascism – also stands for an ideal or rather ideals that are persistent today under other banners: the ideal of life as art, the cult of beauty, the fetishism of courage, the dissolution of alienation in ecstatic feelings of community; the repudiation of the intellect; the family of man (under the parenthood of leaders). These ideas are vivid and moving to many people, and it is dishonest as well as tautological to say that one is affected by 'Triumph of the Will' and 'Olympia' only because they are made by a filmmaker of genius."[68]

This is not to say that art by Riefenstahl – or Karadžić – is legitimised by bearing resemblance to art we accept as part of the canon of Western culture. If anything, it is the opposite: if we find Riefenstahl disturbing, it should not be because her aesthetic and content/ 'message' is an aberration of our culture's sensibilities, but precisely because many of her photographs would not look out of place variously in Vogue or a twentieth-century art gallery. Zygmunt Bauman has demonstrated how the first generation of Holocaust historians portrayed the Holocaust as an aberration of Western culture and history, committed by a handful of monsters fundamentally psychologically different from the rest of us, rather than situating the genocide within the broader context out of which it was born.

As Bauman shows[69], this position is both historically inaccurate and morally unhelpful, and a full understanding of such atrocities can only be achieved by understanding how they arose out of a culture – in this case, art – we believe to be 'legitimate'. Hannah Arendt's reports from the Eichmann trial in Jerusalem also instigated a conceptual shift away from the idea that high-level Nazi criminals were fundamentally 'of a different nature' to other people, and thus categorically discrete (although it should be noted that Arendt rejected the fatalist interpretation of her Eichmann trial reports that environments such as Nazi Germany would inevitably lead most people to make the same choices as Eichmann, and she firmly asserted her belief in moral agency and, thus, in responsibility).[70] Fascism and the Holocaust, in other words, were born out of Western culture, and cannot be conceptually cut off from it.

Moreover, when we look beyond Nazi art and genocidal hate speech in particular, it becomes clearer that we can almost never neatly separate discriminatory art – art which has the effect of hate speech – and treat it as a discrete category. In *Culture and Imperialism*, Edward Said outlines how works of colonial-era British literature upheld the project of British imperialism and facilitated the construction of imperial identity and an 'Other'-ing conception of colonised peoples which created a climate whereby institutional global discrimination became acceptable – even in works previously regarded as neutral or domestically apolitical, like Austen's *Mansfield Park*.[71] Moreover, Terry Eagleton, writing on Irish literary traditions, has shown that even literature which intends to respond to/ oppose the exclusivist literature identified by Said does so on the same terms, whether intentionally, through irony, or otherwise.[72] Although they are working within literary theory, Said and Eagleton raise a pertinent question for political philosophers: in light of *Culture and Imperialism*, where would those who believe we must limit free speech at the point of hate speech draw the line when for fascistic, racist and otherwise discriminatory overtones in art – at Wagner, at *Little Black Sambo*, at Shylock?

In the Introduction, I outlined the harm/ offence distinction and the problem of 'explicitness' in the traditional freedom of expression debate, which seemingly has no room to accommodate 'coded' or 'covert' hate speech. The problem these artworks pose is that, while they contain no explicit incitements, nor are they merely offensive in the way Rushdie's novel was: as Said shows, they normalise existing discrimination and construct a climate where social violence against 'Others' becomes acceptable. Karadžić's poetry – implicit, metaphorical, but overwhelmingly ultranationalist – falls into the same problematic category. The traditional debate on freedom of expression has no way to accommodate this grey area.

The second important issue Sontag's essay raises – the question of context – provides a partial solution to this grey area. Sontag berates both traditional art criticism and fashion-preoccupied 'aesthetes' for decontextualising Riefenstahl by locating her work variously within the false neutrality of formalism or viewing it with a camp sensibility which refuses to seriously acknowledge content. She highlights the problem this presents for identifying fascist overtones, leaving the audience vulnerable to absorb their message. She writes: "Riefenstahl's current de-Nazification and vindication as indomitable priestess of the beautiful...does not augur well for the keenness of current sensibilities to detect the fascist longings in our midst. Without a historical perspective, such connoisseurship...prepares the way for a curiously absentminded acceptance of propaganda of all sorts of destructive feelings – feelings whose implications people are refusing to take seriously".[73]

Sontag concludes that "taste is context", that only by continually placing Nazi art in its historical perspective are we safe from perpetuating fascist aesthetics, and therefore fascist ideology. We can see this in Habermas's idea of speech as communicative action: that speech does not perform the same 'act' at all times, but is instead context-specific.[74] In the Introduction, I introduced the idea that hate speech can be defined as speech or symbolic 'speech ' which performs the act of incitement to social violence. Using Habermas's idea, we can reformulate our definition to say that, when the context does not allow the 'act' of incitement to social violence to be performed, the work is no longer hate speech *in that context.*

The idea of context is built into our everyday approach to artistic hate speech. Imagine, for instance, the difference between using Riefenstahl's art in an academic seminar on the role of art in fascist identity and using it gratuitously at a neo-Nazi rally. Our common sense tells us that we cannot make equivalence between the two events, because the context would not allow Riefenstahl's art to perform the same 'act' in both circumstances. On this, we can concede a point in favour of PEN Slovakia's position on Karadžić's poetry: there is no evidence that the journal attempted to contextualise Karadžić's poem so it could not perform the 'act' he originally intended. It could also be recommended that PEN Slovakia would more easily be able to maintain both its commitment to free speech and its concerns over Karadžić's poetry if it had instead recommended that Karadžić's poetry only be presented in a context where it could not perform the act of hate speech.

In conclusion, here I have highlighted two aspects that the traditional debate ignores, the 'bleed' of fascistic art into wider Western culture, and the issue of context. The overlap between fascistic art and art we consider legitimate shows that the traditional debate cannot apply its rubric to art, as it is overly focused on explicit incitement. This is particularly problematic because it is subtle and implicit art like Riefenstahl's and Karadžić's which many people find most moving, and thus has more power to incite them to social violence. The idea of context allows us to modify our definition of hate speech, meaning that even if we support censoring ultranationalist or fascistic art, we do not need to censor it in all contexts.[75] Finally, it is important to acknowledge the limitations of the insight Sontag's work provides on context – while it is an improvement on the traditional debate, it does not provide a comprehensive practical framework, of how exactly to ensure that hate-speech art is always presented in a context which undercuts its power to incite social violence. To complete this picture, and devise a practical approach to artistic hate speech, I will draw upon the capabilities approach.

4.4 Capabilities and hate speech

This sub-chapter will make the case for the policy of 'speaking back', which Gelber has developed out of Nussbaum's capability approach, and then briefly return to Brian Barry's pertinent critique of any 'group rights' practice, to demonstrate how the capabilities approach, when applied to hate speech and freedom of expression, overcomes the potential pitfalls that Brian Barry pointed out in his debates with Bikhu Parekh.

To situate Gelber's theory in its proper context, however, requires a brief reiteration of the capabilities approach and how it relates to human rights theory. As noted in the Introduction, Martha Nussbaum's and Amartya Sen's capability approach was developed to remedy the deficiencies of both utilitarian and Rawlsian social contractarian theories of justice. It is an outcome-oriented theory of justice, which measures the 'justness' of any social arrangement or nation by the extent to which it secures for each individual a list of central 'capabilities' like the ability to live to an old age, the ability to participate in broader politics and culture, and the ability for self-realisation. One advantage of Nussbaum's approach is that it does not measure equality solely in terms of an individual's resources, but in terms of substantive freedoms that would allow a person to pursue the kind of life they desire to, and in this sense it is less open to the criticism of 'prescriptiveness'.

Nussbaum's approach is more distributive than non-interventionist: she asserts that "securing a right to someone requires more than the absence of negative influence."[76] In addition, it does not distinguish between the importance of 'first generation' and 'second generation' rights[77]: whereas Rawls's theory is part of the tradition of believing civil and political rights can come before, and independently of, social, economic and cultural rights, Nussbaum's outcome-oriented approach stresses the need to secure a range of rights simultaneously, in order to ensure individuals a full capacity to pursue their goals.

Applying Nussbaum to hate speech, Katharine Gelber proposes the policy of 'speaking back', which entails providing institutional support to groups who have been harmed by hate speech, giving them public space to refute and respond to derogatory accusations and negative depictions of their group. This builds upon Nussbaum's approach[78] as it acknowledges that hate speech limits the capacities of those who are maligned by it. Gelber notes that one of the harms of hate speech is its 'silencing' effect on the disadvantaged group, as it creates a climate in which members of the targeted group no longer feel able to verbally defend themselves.

Gelber's idea of a forum for 'speaking back' can be interpreted as a group right, inasmuch as the forum would be provided for members of a targeted group, rather than individuals harmed by, for instance, defamation or libel, which judicial systems already accommodate.[79] The policy is aimed at changing the cultural climate so that hate speech cannot become acceptable, as those who propagate it would realise that their hateful depictions and statements would not be allowed to dominate social discourse, and the potency and legitimacy of hate speech would be undermined in the eyes of the intended audience.

I would propose that we combine the 'speaking back' policy with the idea of context developed in the previous sub-chapters: if Riefenstahl's films are screened at, for instance, an ultranationalist or anti-Semitic rally, ensuring that the society's Jewish community had adequate space and support to address the intended audience of the film would undermine much of the power of Riefenstahl's film, which would no longer be able to perform the 'act' it intended, of presenting – without interruption or contradiction – an appealing, aesthetically-pleasing fascistic worldview. In other words, the forum of 'speaking back' in some ways contextualises hate speech, negating its power to convince.

Combined with the idea of context, Gelber's proposal is a helpful contribution to the hate speech debate, for several reasons. Firstly, it solves the problem of the traditional debate in which the need to combat the harm of hate speech and the need to protect free speech are seen as conflicting concerns.

In Gelber's approach, instead of resorting to either censorship or acceptance of the inevitability of hate speech, hate speech is tackled *with* free speech. This also takes us some way toward solving the dilemma posed by Sontag and the 'bleed' of fascistic art into broader culture, as we would no longer have to undertake the impossible task of divining when the line is crossed in art. That Gelber's approach aims to combat effects of hate speech, rather than focusing on what is or is not permissible for someone to say, makes it particularly helpful for artistic hate speech, because – as the analysis of Karadžić's poetry above has indicated – subtle, implicit art can have a 'hate speech effect' though the 'message' is harder to discern. Most fundamentally, Gelber's approach has the advantage of providing a way to be pro-free speech which nonetheless recognises the gravity of harm done by hate speech, rather than dismissing it as the inevitable collateral of upholding the free-speech principle.

Having established the advantages of Gelber's approach over the traditional debate, it remains to acknowledge one major potential criticism. As noted earlier in this work, Brian Barry provides a convincing counter-argument to Kymlicka and Parekh's multiculturalism, as he demonstrates that group rights can be used to oppress individuals, undermining both liberty and equality. Barry's position poses the question: if we allow a 'group right' mechanism – such as a forum for a disadvantaged group, as a group, to 'speak back' against hate speech – would it lead to groups oppressing or silencing individuals through 'group definition', such as Rushdie's persecution after *The Satanic Verses*? As stated earlier, Parekh commented in the wake of the Rushdie controversy that the liberal defense of Rushdie's free speech was patronising and mistakenly proposed that society could be modelled on a 'marketplace of ideas', in which, Parekh argues, minority cultures and beliefs would be marginalised or become extinct due to the *de facto* cultural tyranny of the majority.[80] Barry, meanwhile, responded[81] by noting that Parekh's schema would give self-defined 'groups' the right to oppress individuals who they labelled to be a member of their group – such as Rushdie being labelled a member of the Muslim community and therefore subject to the rulings of self-appointed 'moral spokespersons' within that community, who used this position to condemn him. (This is not to say that the media establishment in Britain didn't *use* the Rushdie case to perpetuate stereotypes about British Muslims as fundamentalists: Parekh has a valid point on this, but it is a separate issue from the question of whether or not Rushdie should have been allowed to publish *The Satanic Verses*.)

Whilst Barry's criticism deserves recognition – like Waldron's cosmopolitan alternative, it reminds us of the very tangible potential pitfalls in asserting any kind of group rights, lest they deny the transgressive voices within culture and elevate the group over the rights of the individual – Gelber's idea of 'speaking back' can be formulated in such a way to overcome this potential criticism. Firstly, as has been stated throughout, this approach applies only to literary or artistic hate speech which would do tangible harm to a disadvantaged minority, such as Karadžić's poetry, Riefenstahl's films, or *Jud Süss* – not those which, like Rushdie's work, are considered by some to be offensive.

Relatedly, under Gelber's 'speaking back' policy, Rushdie would still have been able to freely publish *The Satanic Verses* without fear of retaliation, as the 'speaking back' position is fundamentally pro-free speech, and ultimately acts as an alternative to censorship. Thirdly, it should be noted that the 'speaking back' position is highly compatible with the idea of 'transgressive voices' and the 'minority within the minority' that I outlined by building upon Gayatri Chakravorty Spivak and Judith Butler's work in Chapter 1, and that this idea of supporting the vital role of transgressive and subversive voices within a community, including minority communities, also allows us to navigate between Barry and Parekh's positions on individual versus group rights. Lastly, it should be stated in case it is not clear, that Gelber's 'speaking back' forum idea is intended to operate as one small component within a liberal, democratic society in which individual rights are fully upheld, and in which all individuals can fully enjoy all their human rights and civil liberties.

In conclusion, this Chapter has shown that drawing upon Nussbaum's capabilities approach allows us to build a position on hate speech and art which neither resorts to censorship nor declares that nothing can be done about the harmful effects of hate speech. The idea of 'speaking back', taken together with the importance of context, indicates a more helpful position on Karadžić's poetry than either PEN Slovakia or the journal that published it. We can conclude that both organisations should

73

have ensured to the best of their ability that the poetry was only published in a context that negated its power to perform the act of hate speech, both in terms of how it was presented in the journal, and the place it occupied in broader public discourse (in other words, its publication necessitated political and civil society to provide an opportunity in media and public space for those harmed by Karadžić's hate speech to respond).

As PEN's stated ethos is to provide a forum for persecuted writers, focusing on this role would be a better way for PEN to combat hate speech in art than advocating censorship of Karadžić's poetry. However, as this Chapter has shown, a pro-free speech position does not mean accepting that nothing can be done about hate speech – it simply means that free speech itself, 'speaking back', must be used as the mechanism for combatting hate speech's harmful effects.

Conclusion

In the preceding Chapters I have built the argument that freedom of literary expression is not only a civil and political right, belonging to the individuals that exercise in their capacity as individual writers, but also an economic, social and cultural right pertaining to the right to access and enjoy culture. Consequently, stifling literary freedom – which can take the form of censorship, a cultural climate of self-censorship, or in various ways of making literature inaccessible to the general populace – is a violation of the right to access and participate in cultural life. This position is premised on the capabilities approach, and thus entails a comprehensive reworking of the idea of securing literary freedom, which has traditionally been seen as a civil and political, or 'first generation' right.

Chapter 1 presented the arguments within contemporary political philosophy that individual identity is not meaningfully divisible from its wider culture, and that culture must therefore be comprehensively protected, and that this protection entails rights that belong to the group as a whole. Moreover, recognising that 'transgressive' voices are an integral part of culture prevents the philosophical impasse of Brian Barry's argument against Bikhu Parekh, that group rights oppress the individual.

Chapter 2 argued that it is imperative that the state fund 'high art' such as contemporary literature, not because 'high art' is juxtaposed with Adorno's idea of the "culture industry" of popular culture, but because, according to the capabilities approach, each individual in a society must have access to a full range of choices in order to have meaningful freedom, and that securing this entails simultaneously ensuring numerous core 'entitlements' such as education, healthcare, and the ability to enjoy one's culture.

Chapter 3 then addressed the interrelationship between the

writer and society, and the complexity of the idea of the 'group' in the face of the concept that literature transcends borders/ nations/ culture: examining the relation between the writer and society informs our understanding of what kind of state support there should be for literature (and the arts in general), so that it does not become a mechanism of state ideology or the majority.

Taken together, this builds the case for conceiving of literary freedom as a cultural right. Chapter 4 completes the most striking 'missing piece' in the argument that literary freedom is a cultural right, by addressing the issue of literary hate speech, and demonstrating how a capabilities approach, and a pro-free speech position of 'speaking back'– itself an assertion of cultural rights – provides a way of dealing with literary hate speech which avoids the pitfalls of the traditional approach to freedom of expression posited by J. S. Mill and others.

I would like to acknowledge here that the argument I have presented has numerous limitations, most of which relate to its application of the capabilities approach. As the academic analysis of the capabilities approach has generally been concerned with applying its insights to issues such as healthcare, building a capabilities-based position on literary freedom entailed missing out many important aspects of Sen and Nussbaum's analysis. In particular, as Sen and Nussbaum stress that expanding people's capacity for fulfilled and meaningful lives requires securing many rights/ entitlements simultaneously, it follows that economic, social and cultural rights, and civil and political rights are mutually reinforcing. While this is a helpful insight, it leaves many unexplored issues here, such as the ways in which, for instance, securing certain economic rights would improve people's lives in another area, such as the entitlement to participate in culture.

While literacy and education are clearly particularly central to ensuring individuals can exercise their right to participate in and enjoy culture, Sen and Nussbaum's argument is that we should treat all key entitlements as equally important, and equally inter-related, to leading a fulfilling life. A more detailed study would be able to explore more aspects of interrelated rights/ entitle-ments.

A second limitation has been the focus here on the nexus of: writer (or individual) – society – the *state*. In particular, the recommendations on positive steps to be taken to secure the meaningful practice of literary freedom has been addressed to 'the state'.

In her work on 'frontiers of justice', however, Nussbaum has argued that the capabilities approach is premised on the idea that obligation in ensuring entitlements falls not only to states, who must secure these for all their citizens, or all inhabitants, but that these obligations fall to "humanity in general."[82] Transnational obligations in securing economic, social and cultural rights has very tangible contemporary relevance due to extreme continued global inequalities. A clear point for further research, then, on literary freedom as a cultural right, is on the transnational implications once concrete measures required to secure literary freedom have been identified.

Similarly, it was beyond the remit of my work here to fully explore the question of whether an emphasis on literary culture is by definition Eurocentric, or privileges cultures with literary traditions over cultures which emphasise oral traditions. A more thorough examination of this question would have been able to more fully arguments by post-colonial literary theorists such as Said and Bhabha, that argue both that the Eurocentric 'canon' has been privileged over other equally valid forms of art and story-telling, but simultaneously that great art – including great literature – belongs to the world as a whole.

One last major point for further research stems from an explo-ration of difference, and how this applies to the issue of literary censorship within a society. The concept of 'censorship' has been taken, for the purposes of my argument here, to mean a blanket ban (of, for instance, a novel) across the whole of the state – and thus equally affecting all citizens, at least indirectly by altering the cultural climate, as outlined in the case of post-1968 Czechoslovakia. In most traditional analysis of freedom of expression, from J.S. Mill onwards, there is a latent assumption that censoring authorities do not wish for *any* citizen to read a work that is deemed, in the eyes of the state/ authorities, to be undesirable; this assumption has also been held through my analysis here.

Such a position, however, falls apart when we begin to look at the different ways literary censorship has been advocated, sometimes including a discriminatory paternalism towards certain sections of a society in particular. The often-cited rhetorical comment of the prosecution counsel, Mervyn Griffith-Jones, at the D.H. Lawrence obscenity trial was: "is [*Lady Chatterley's Lover*] a book you would wish your wife or servants to read?"[83] – implying that, while the middle-class Englishmen in the court-room might not find Lawrence's novel offensive or obscene, they have the right, and the paternalistic 'duty', to think on behalf of – and make the decision of censorship on behalf of – disadvantaged members of society (namely, the working-class and women) who were presumed incapable of adequately making this decision for themselves. This example indicates that, to have a comprehensive approach to securing literary freedom and access to culture, we must take into account prevailing modes of discriminations within a society, and ensure that these modes of discrimination are not mirrored in the state's conception of who, within the society, constitutes the 'ideal reader.'

Another area where this clearly presents itself is in the issue of literary translation into minority languages, in order to ensure that national minorities have the choice to enjoy the literature of the dominant culture if they choose to do so. While this is clearly one of the important areas to highlight in presenting the case for literary freedom as a cultural right, opening this box entails a full analysis that of issues associated with linguistic rights, and with the concept of what constitutes a 'national minority', is subject to much analysis in academic theory on economic, social and cultural rights. Further research on this topic could entail examining the interrelation between language rights and access to 'high art.'

Furthermore, there are several key areas left unexplored in my application of capabilities theory to hate speech. Firstly, I have focused on literature or, (in the case of Riefenstahl) art, which reinforced and constructed Nazi or 'Milošević-ian' world-views, but a broader study could include art from a wider variety of regimes, including analysis of variance in how different regimes have used literature and art, as the manner in which literature and art has been utilised by exclusivist doctrines undoubtedly changes significantly dependent on the place, time, and context. Another area left to be explored in my analysis of literary hate speech is hate speech in which the incitement is not towards a national/ ethnic/ religious group such as Jews or Bosnian Muslims, but towards, for instance, women – gender as a unit of analysis is notably lacking from the debate on hate speech, yet gender remains one of the pervasive grounds of discrimination worldwide. Thirdly, the topic of hate speech and art raises theoretical points which were beyond the scope of this study, such as the philosophical dilemma of what to do about 'hate speech that fails to incite', where the speech does not manage to attract an audience to its message – this raises the question, for instance, of whether the duty to mitigate against the damage done by (literary) hate speech is only present when the hate speech is 'effective', widely disseminated, and so on.

Lastly, as our understanding of hate speech – literary and otherwise – develops, there is a corresponding need to ensure legal protections of hate speech are developed: as noted in the Introduction, hate speech legislation is overwhelmingly framed in 'incitement to racial hatred' terms, which excludes incitement to homophobic and misogynist hate-crimes. Changing our conception of the way hate speech harms others, and on which identity-lines, is essential to addressing the problem. Chapter 4 pointed towards the frameworks required to address hate speech, but more extensive work is clearly needed on how 'speaking back' forums would work. On the other hand, more than simply focusing on developing frameworks and legal norms, I intended to demonstrate that the issue of hate speech, particularly 'covert' and literary hate speech, also requires a change in attitude: one of the main benefits of a 'speaking back' approach is that, unlike the traditional debate, it constructs a pro-free speech position that fully acknowledges the devastating damage that hate speech can cause. A pro-free speech approach to hate speech which also acknowledges its seriousness and mitigates its worst effects is a starting point for fostering a culture of 'speaking back' in which hate speech would lose its potency and power to harm.

Nonetheless, despite the significant limitations of this study, I have attempted to show that access to literature, and a holistic approach to literary freedom that notes the social role of the writer, the detrimental effects of self-censorship, and provides a way to deal with literary hate speech, is both an important issue in its own right, and a lens through which to demonstrate the interrelated nature of 'first' and 'second' generation rights. This has been asserted throughout by demonstrating the relevance and appropriateness of the capabilities approach to dealing with this issue, which has heretofore been addressed predominantly as an issue of 'civil and political rights'. As well as highlighting the importance of literary freedom and access to literature/ art, my central claim here is an assertion that human rights are not meaningful unless positive actions are take by states and similar actors to secure them for everyone, and that there is a moral imperative on relevant bodies of power to do so.

Bibliography

Primary Sources

Adorno, Theodor. *The Culture Industry: Selected Essays on Mass Culture.* Routledge Classics reprint. London, UK. 2001.

Anderson, Benedict. *Imagined Communities: Reflections on the Origin and Spread of Nationalism.* Verso Publishers. London, United Kingdom. 1991.

Article 19 Freedom of Expression Manual. *International and Comparative Law Standards and Procedures.* The Bath Press. Avon, UK. 1993.

Berlin, Isaiah. 'Two Concepts of Liberty.' 1958. *Four Essays on Liberty.* Oxford University Press. Oxford, UK. 1969.

Bhabha, Homi. *The Location of Culture.* Routledge. London, UK. 1994.

Butler, Judith and Gayatri Spivak. *Who Sings The Nation State?* Seagull Books. New York, USA. 2007.

Culik, Jan. 'Czech Literature and the Reading Public.' Lecture given at the *Glasgow Igor Hajek Memorial Conference.* 1995. http://www.arts.gla.ac.uk/Slavonic/staff/Czech_literature.ht m (Accessed September 10th 2010).

Gellner, Ernst. *Nations and Nationalism.* Cornell University Press. Ithaca, NY, USA. 1983.

Gutthy, Agnieszka (ed). *Literature in Exile of Eastern and Central Europe. Peter* Lang Publishers. New York, USA. 2009.

Hobsbawm, Eric and Terence Ranger. *The Invention of Tradition.* Canto, Cambridge University Press. Cambridge, United Kingdom. 1983.

Human Rights Education Associates. *International Legal Protection of Freedom of Expression.* http://www.hrea. org/index.php?base_id=147 (Accessed September 2nd 2010).

International PEN. *Freedom of Expression.* http://www.interna-tionalpen.org.uk/go/freedom-of-expression

Kymlicka, Will. 'The Value of Cultural Membership' in *Liberalism, Community and Culture*. Clarendon Press. Oxford, United Kingdom. 1991.

Nussbaum, Martha. *Frontiers of Justice: Disability, Nationality, Species Membership*. Harvard University Press. Cambridge, USA. 2006.

Nussbaum, Martha and Amartya Sen (eds). *The Quality of Life*. Clarendon Press. Oxford, UK. 1993.

Orwell, George. 'The Freedom of the Press'. Intended to be used as preface for the first edition of *Animal Farm*, 1946. http://michaelbryson.net/teaching/csun/orwell.pdf (Accessed 15th August 2010).

Sontag, Susan. 'Fascinating Fascism'. New York Review of Books, Vol 22, No 1. Feb 1975.

Waldron, Jeremy. 'Minority Cultures and the Cosmopolitan Alternative' in Kymlicka, W (ed) *The Rights of Minority Cultures*. Oxford University Press. Oxford, UK. 1995.

Young, I. M. 'Social Movements and the Politics of Difference' in *Justice and the Politics of Difference*. Princeton University Press. New Jersey, USA. 1990.

Secondary Sources

Achebe, Chinua. 'The Role of the Writer in a New Nation.' Text of a lecture at the Nigerian Library Association. *Nigerian Magazine*, No. 81, June 1964. p157-160.

Althusser, Louis. 'Ideology and Ideological State Apparatus.' (1971) Republished in *Lenin and Philosophy, and Other Essays*. Monthly Review Press. New York, USA. 2001.

Anand P, Santos C and Smith R. "The Measurements of Capabilities" in *Arguments for a Better World: Essays in Honor of Amartya Sen*. Basu K and R Kanbur, eds. Oxford University Press. Oxford, United Kingdom. 2009.

Arnold, Matthew. *Culture and Anarchy: Rethinking the Western Tradition*. First published 1869. Yale University Press. New

Haven, USA. 1994.

Arendt, Hannah. *Eichmann in Jerusalem: A Report on the Banality of Evil*. Penguin reissued edition. London, United Kingdom. 1993.

Appignanesi, Lisa and Sara Maitland, eds. *The Rushdie Files*. Fourth Estate Publishers. London, United Kingdom. 1989.

Barthes, Roland. 'The Death of the Author' in *Image, Music, Text*. Translated by Stephen Heath. Hill and Wang Publishers. New York, USA. 1978. Essay also available online at http://evans-experientialism.freewebspace.com/barthes06.htm (Accessed 12th September 2010).

Bauman, Zygmunt. *Modernity and the Holocaust*. Cornell University Press. Ithaca, NY, USA. 1989.

Carroll, David. *French Literary Fascism: Nationalism, Anti-Semitism and the Ideology of Culture*. Princeton University Press. New Jersey, USA. 1994.

Casanova, Pascale. *The World Republic of Letters*. Harvard University Press. Cambridge, MA, USA. 2004.

Coliver, Sandra, ed. *Striking a Balance: Hate Speech, Freedom of Expression and Non-Discrimination*. ARTICLE 19 and Human Rights Centre, University of Essex. Essex and London, United Kingdom.1992.

Damrosch, David. *What Is World Literature?* Princeton University Press. New Jersey, USA. 2003.

Eagleton, Terry, Fredric Jameson and Edward Said. *Nationalism, Colonialism and Literature*. University of Minnesota Press. Minneapolis, USA. 1990.

Edmondson, Henry T. *The Moral of the Story: Literature and Public Ethics*. Lexington Books. New York, USA.

English PEN. *Writers in Prison*. http://www.englishpen.org /writersinprison/statistics/ (accessed 16th September 2010).

Gelber, Katharine. *Speaking Back: the Free Speech versus Hate Speech Debate*. John Benjamin Publishers. Philadelphia, USA. 2002.

Habermas, Jürgen. *Theory of Communicative Action*. Polity Press. Cambridge, UK. 1987.

Holy, Jiri. *Writers Under Siege: Czech Literature since 1945*. Sussex Academic Press. Sussex, UK. 2007.

Hudson, Robert. "Songs of Seduction: Popular Music and Serbian Nationalism." *Patterns of Prejudice* Vol 37, No 2. 2003.

Lipstadt, Deborah. 'Even a 'remake' of *Jud Süss* can never be neutral.' *The Guardian* newspaper. 5th October 2010. Available online at http://www.guardian.co.uk/commentisfree/2010/oct/05/jud-suss-goebbels-remake-germany. (Accessed 5th October 2010).

Marcuse, Herbert. *Eros and Civilisation: A Philosophical Inquiry into Freud*. First published 1956. Reissued in English by Routledge Press. Oxford, UK. 1998.

McRobie, Heather. 'Karadžić , Riefenstahl and Rushdie' in *Novi Pogledi* Vol 16. ACIPS, University of Sarajevo. 15th March 2010.

McRobie, Heather. 'Should PEN condemn Radovan Karadžić 's poetry?' *The Guardian* newspaper. 15th April 2009. Available online at http://www.guardian.co.uk/books/booksblog/2009/apr/15/1. (Accessed October 5th 2010).

Mill, J.S. *On Liberty and Other Writings*. Collini, Stephan ed. Cambridge University Press reprint. Cambridge, United Kingdom. 2001.

Nussbaum, Martha. *Frontiers of Justice: Disability, Nationality, Species Membership*. Harvard University Press. Cambridge, Massachusetts, USA. 2006.

Nussbaum, Martha. *Hiding From Humanity: Disgust, Shame and the Law*. Princeton University Press. New Jersey, USA. 2004.

Orwell, George. 'Politics and the English Language'. 1946. Available online at http://mla.stanford.edu/Politics_&_English_language.pdf (Accessed 12th September 2010).

Parekh, Bikhu. *Rethinking Multiculturalism: Cultural Diversity and Political Theory*. London: Palgrave Macmillan. 2006.

Rubin, Andrew. "The Executioner's Song." *Lingua Franca*. July

1995.

Said, Edward. *Culture and Imperialism*. Vintage. London, United Kingdom. 1993.

Sennett, Richard. *The Fall of Public Man*. Cambridge University Press. Cambridge, United Kingdom. 1974.

Shigeno, Rei. 'Nationalism and Serbian Intellectuals.' *Perspectives on European Politics and Society*. Vol 15, Issue 1. 2004.

Soyinka, Wole. 'Voices from the frontier: writers in exile.' *The Guardian* newspaper, 13th July 2002. http://www.guardian.co.uk/books/2002/jul/13/poetry.wolesoyinka (Accessed 5th October 2010).

Surdukowski, Jay. "Is Poetry a War Crime?: Reckoning for Radovan Karadžić the Poet Warrior." *Michigan Journal of International Law*, Vol 47. July 2005.

Swann, Susan. 'The Writer's Conscience.' Speech at the Annual Robarts Lecture, York University, Toronto, Canada. 2000.

Shiach, Morag. 'To Purify the Dialect of the Tribe.' *Modernism and Language Reform Journal*. Volume 14, Number 1, January 2007.

Trilling, Lionel. *Sincerity and Authenticity*. Harvard University Press. Cambridge, Massachssuetts, USA. 1972.

Tsesis, Alexander. *Destructive Messages: How Hate Speech Paves the Way for Harmful Social Movements*. New York University Press. New York, USA. 2002.

Voloshinov, Valentin. *Marxism and the Philosophy of Language*. Harvard University Press. Cambridge, Massachssuetts, USA. 1986.

von Kunes, Karen. 'The National Paradox: Czech Literature and the Gentle Revolution' in *World Literature Today*, Vol 65., No. 2. University of Oklahoma Press. Oklahoma, USA. 1991.

Waluchow, Wilfred (ed). *Free Expression: Essays in Law and Philosophy*. Clarendon Press. Oxford, United Kingdom. 1994.

Westerman, Frank. *Engineers of the Soul: in the Footsteps of Stalin's Writers*. Harvill Secker. London, United Kingdom. 2010.

Endnotes

1. Culik, Jan. 'Czech Literature and the Reading Public.' Lecture given at the Glasgow Igor Hajek Memorial Conference. 1995. http://www.arts.gla.ac.uk/Slavonic/staff/ Czech_literature.html (Accessed 5th October 2010).

2. Culik, Jan. 'Czech Literature and the Reading Public.'

3. English PEN. *Writers in Prison.* http://www.englishpen .org/writersinprison/statistics (Accessed 5th October 2010).

4. PEN's national chapters, such as PEN Slovakia, are semi-autonomous sections of PEN International, an independent non-governmental organisation which was founded in 1921. PEN International states that its purpose is to protect the "freedom to express ideas without fear of attack, arrest or other persecution" and it asserts that "everyone has the right to freedom of expression; this right includes freedom to hold opinions without interference and to seek, receive, and impart information and ideas through any media and regardless of frontiers" and this statement of intent is also subscribed to by all national chapters, such as PEN Slovakia, when they found their branch of the organization. See International PEN. *Freedom of Expression.* http://www. internationalpen.org.uk/go/freedom-of-expression

5. McRobie, Heather. 'Should PEN condemn Radovan Karadžić's poetry?' *The Guardian* newspaper. 15th April 2009. Available online at http://www.guardian.co.uk/books/books blog/2009/apr/15/1. (Accessed October 5th 2010).

6. Human Rights Education Associates. International Legal Protection of Freedom of Expression. http://www.hrea.org /index.php?base_id=147 (Accessed September 10th 2010).

7. One way to demonstrate the issue of artistic merit and freedom of speech would be by a comparison between the 2008 *The Jewel of Medina* novel controversy and *The Satanic*

Verses controversy. Sherry Jones's novel *The Jewel of Medina*, which re-imagines reimagines the life of the Prophet Muhammad's bride Aisha, was widely criticised on literary grounds by commentators to be a sub-standard, artistically unoriginal and essentialist "historical-romance". Nonetheless, the content of the novel — depicting figures of religious importance such as the Prophet Muhammad in a complex, imperfect and perhaps derogatory light — was substantively similar to Rushdie's *The Satanic Verses*, which many literary critics find to be original, nuanced, artistically accomplished and so on. It follows that, if we are to defend Rushdie's right to publish *The Satanic Verses* without fear of persecution, we must also defend Sherry Jones's right to publish *The Jewel of Medina*, regardless of the fact it almost certainly contributes far less to the canon of world literature than Rushdie.

8. Please note that the "Freedom of Expression" part of the Introduction has been developed out of an article I wrote that was then published in the University of Sarajevo's *Novi Pogledi* magazine in March 2010, and there are some overlaps between the content of the published article and the work I am presenting here. Please see: McRobie, Heather. 'Karadžić, Riefenstahl and Rushdie' in *Novi Pogledi* Vol 16. ACIPS, University of Sarajevo. 15th March 2010.

9. Raz, Joseph. 'Free Expression and Personal Identification', in Waluchow, Wilfred, ed. *Free Expression: Essays in Law and Philosophy*. Clarendon Press. Oxford, UK. 1994

10. Richards, David J. 'Free Speech as Toleration', in Waluchow, Wilfred, ed. *Free Expression: Essays in Law and Philosophy*.

11. McRobie, Heather. 'Karadžić, Riefenstahl and Rushdie' in *Novi Pogledi* Vol 16. ACIPS, University of Sarajevo. 15th March 2010.

12. *Introduction*, Appignanesi, Lisa and Sara Maitland, eds. *The Rushdie Files*. 4th Estate Publishers. London, UK. 1989.

13. Nussbaum, Martha. *Hiding From Humanity: Disgust, Shame and the Law.* Princeton University Press. Princeton, New Jersey, USA. 2004.

14. Narveson, Jan. 'Freedom of Speech and Expression: A Libertarian View' in Waluchow, Wilfred, ed. *Free Expression: Essays in Law and Philosophy.* Clarendon Press. Oxford, UK. 1994.

15. From the original "everyone has the right to say anything he or she wishes", Narveson reformulates it to "everyone has the right to say anything he or she wishes to anyone who is willing to hear that speech-act, provided (1) no third-parties are made unwilling recipients of unwarranted messages and (2) that the speeches in question are not in context means to visiting uncompensated costs on [i.e. harming] any third parties." Narveson, Jan. p.71.

16. Narveson, Jan. p.85.

17. Nussbaum, Martha. *Frontiers of Justice: Disability, Nationality, Species Membership.* Harvard University Press. Cambridge, USA. 2006. p.288

18. Nussbaum notes that "people often learn not to want things that convention and political realities have put beyond their reach...we observe it particularly often in women's aspirations, which adjust to time-sanctioned depictions of a woman's proper role, a woman's bodily weakness, and so forth". Therefore preference-based approaches such as utilitarianism and Rawls's theory of justice often end up supporting an unjust status quo. The capabilities approach avoids this pitfall, and is thus more able to lead to the development of a just society, as it is concerned with developing capabilities so that no person's choices are limited by what society has taught them is impossible for disadvantaged members to achieve. Nussbaum, Martha. *Frontiers of Justice.* p.283.

19. Illustrative of the endless task of striking upon an exhaustive

definition of the word "culture" is the fact that Alfred Kroeber and Clyde Kluckhohn were able to list over 150 definitions of the word in their book *Culture: A Critical Review of Concepts and Definitions.* See Kroeber, A and Clyde Kluckhohn, *Culture: A Critical Review of Concepts and Definitions.* University of Virginia Press. Virginia, USA. 1978.

20. Anderson, Benedict. *Imagined Communities: Reflections on the Origin and Spread of Nationalism.* Verso Publishers. London, United Kingdom. 1991. p4.

21. Hobsbawm, Eric and Terence Ranger. *The Invention of Tradition.* Canto, Cambridge University Press. Cambridge, United Kingdom. 1983.

22. Waldron, Jeremy. 'Minority Cultures and the Cosmopolitan Alternative.' in Kymlicka, W (ed) *The Rights of Minority Cultures.* Oxford University Press. Oxford, UK. 1995. p99.

23. It is worth quoting Bhabha's description of 'elite' cosmopolitanism, which he juxtaposes against his own conception of a more egalitarian 'vernacular cosmopolitanism', the description of the former vividly recalls Waldron's vision of an individual rights-based multiculturalism: "There is a kind of global cosmopolitanism...that configures the planet as a concentric world of national societies extending to global villages. It is a cosmopolitanism of relative prosperity and privilege founded on ideas of governance that are complicit with free-market forms of governance, and free-market forces of competition...A global cosmopolitanism of this sort readily celebrates a world of plural cultures and peoples located at the periphery, so long as they produce healthy profit margins within metropolitan societies. In celebrating a 'world culture' or 'world markets' this mode of cosmopolitanism moves swiftly and selectively from one island of prosperity to yet another terrain of technological productivity, paying conspicuously less attention to the persistent inequality and immiseration produced by such

unequal and uneven development." Bhabha, Homi. *The Location of Culture*. Routledge. London, UK. 1994, p.xiv.

24. Waldron, Jeremy. 'Minority Cultures and the Cosmopolitan Alternative.' p107.

25. Waldron, Jeremy. p102.

26. Bhabha, Homi. *The Location of Culture*. Routledge. p83.

27. Kymlicka, Will. 'The Value of Cultural Membership. in *Liberalism, Community and Culture*. Clarendon Press. Oxford, UK. 1991. p105.

28. Young, I. M. 'Social Movements and the Politics of Difference' in *Justice and the Politics of Difference*. Princeton University Press. New Jersey, USA. 1990. p158.

29. Young, I.M. p164.

30. Young, I.M. p166.

31. Butler, Judith and Gayatri Spivak. *Who Sings The Nation State?* Seagull Books. New York, USA. 2007. p36.

32. Adorno, Theodor. *The Culture Industry: Selected Essays on Mass Culture*. Routledge Classics reprint. London, UK. 2001.

33. Gramsci's development of the idea of 'cultural hegemony', and his thesis that cultural norms should not be perceived as 'neutral' or inevitable' but instead a means through which different classes or groups vie for power over society as a whole, would have been an equally valid lens through which to make this case regarding 'high art', however, Adorno's work more closely fits with the focus of my analysis here as it is particularly concerned with literature and other artistic works, rather than 'culture' as a whole.

34. Adorno, Theodor. *The Culture Industry: Selected Essays on Mass Culture*. p61.

35. Adorno, Theodor. p63.

36. In *Eros and Civilisation*, Marcuse builds upon both Marx and Freud to outline a vision of an emancipated society, much as Adorno outlines emancipation from the 'culture industry'. Marcuse departs from Marx in conceiving of history not in

terms of an entrenched class struggle but instead – and here Marcuse allies with Freud – as a struggle against our natural instincts and desires. However, Marcuse concurs with Marx that it is under capitalism and contemporary industrialised society that people are alienated from their true self, whilst disagreeing with Freud that repression is 'necessary' for functional and 'civilised' societal life. Marcuse thus envisions societal emancipation in terms of liberation from the repression of our natural instincts and desires. As another member of the Frankfurt School, Marcuse's understanding of emancipation is relevant here as it informs Adorno's conception of 'emancipation' from the culture industry through the true pleasures – in Adorno's analysis, the true pleasures brought by high art. See: Marcuse, Herbert. *Eros and Civilisation: A Philosophical Inquiry into Freud.* First published 1956. Reissued in English by Routledge Press. Oxford, UK. 1998.

37. Althusser, Louis. 'Ideology and Ideological State Apparatus.' (1971) Republished in *Lenin and Philosophy, and Other Essays.* Monthly Review Press. New York, USA. 2001. p158-9.

38. Frank Westerman notes that Stalin coined the phrase 'engineers of the human soul' to describe writers at a state reception 'greeting' Soviet novelists and playwrights. Westerman details how Maxim Gorky advised Stalin on the most effective methods for 'utilising' literature for the USSR's ends, and the manner in which socialist realism was constructed by Soviet politicans, although he notes that key writers played an active and willing role in aiding its development. See Westerman, Frank. *Engineers of the Soul: in the Footsteps of Stalin's Writers.* Harvill Secker. London, UK. 2010.

39. Voloshinov, Valentin. *Marxism and the Philosophy of Language.* Harvard University Press. Harvard, USA. 1986.

40. Shiach, Morag. 'To Purify the Dialect of the Tribe.' *Modernism and Language Reform Journal.* Volume 14, Number 1, January 2007. p21-34.

41. Barthes, Roland. Ibid. 'The Death of the Author' in *Image, Music, Text.* Translated by Stephen Heath. Hill and Wang Publishers. New York, USA. 1978. Essay also available online at http://evans-experientialism.freewebspace.com/barthes0 6.htm (Accessed 5th October 2010).

42. Barthes, Roland. Ibid. 'The Death of the Author' in *Image, Music, Text.*

43. Barthes, Roland. 'The Death of the Author' in *Image, Music, Text.*

44. Barthes, Roland. Ibid.

45. Trilling, Lionel. *Sincerity and Authenticity.* Harvard University Press. Cambridge, Massachssuetts, USA. 1972. p8.

46. Sennett, Richard. *The Fall of Public Man.* Cambridge University Press. Cambridge, United Kingdom. 1974.

47. The term 'moral imagination' is worthy of further examination, as it has been utilised by different theorists in different ways. Many attribute the phrase to the British conservative thinker Edmund Burke, but more recent scholars such as Martha Nussbaum have used the term to incorporate the 'non-rational' into the political philosophy discussion of human rights, particularly in her assertion of the legitimate role of empathy in informing our understanding of human rights.

48. Swann, Susan. 'The Writer's Conscience.' Speech at the Annual Robarts Lecture, York University, Toronto, Canada. 2000.

49. Achebe, Chinua. 'The Role of the Writer in a New Nation.' Text of a lecture at the Nigerian Library Association. Nigerian Magazine, No. 81, June 1964. p157-160.

50. Orwell, George. 'The Freedom of the Press'. Intended to be used as preface for the first edition of *Animal Farm*, 1946.

51. Culik, Jan. 'Czech Literature and the Reading Public.' Lecture given at the Glasgow Igor Hajek Memorial Conference. 1995. http://www.arts.gla.ac.uk/Slavonic/staff/Czech_literature.htm (Accessed 5th October 2010).

52. Soyinka, Wole. 'Voices from the frontier: writers in exile.' The Guardian newspaper, 13th July 2002. http://www.guardian.co.uk/books/2002/jul/13/poetry.wolesoyinka (Accessed 5th October 2010).

53. Damrosch, David. *What Is World Literature?* Princeton University Press. New Jersey, USA. 2003.

54. Casanova, Pascale. *The World Republic of Letters*. Harvard University Press. Cambridge, USA. 2004. p40.

55. As noted earlier, Katherine Gelber's application of Nussbaum and Habermas to Australian hate speech legislation is one exception to this, and an interestng use of capabilities theory, but does not concern itself in particular with hate speech which is articulated through literature.

56. Damrosch makes the interesting argument that our current understanding of the concept of 'world literature' is most severely lacking when it comes to incorporating the concept of time: "All too often, students of imperialism, colonialism, nationalism and globalisation...define their topics in such a way as to restrict their investigations to just the last five hundred years of human history...or even the last few years [leading to an] insistent *presentism* that erases the past as a serious factor, leaving at best a few nostalgic postmodern references." These references will be as misplaced and thoughtless "as the 'local colour' tipped in to distinguish the lobby of the Jakarta Hilton from that of its Cancun counterpart. Not only does this *presentism* deprive us of the ability to learn from a much wider range of empires, colonies, polities, and migrations; it also leaves out of account the dramatic ways in which the canons of the earlier periods themselves are being reshaped through new

attention to all sorts of long-neglected but utterly fascinating texts." Damrosch. p71.

57. See International PEN. *Freedom of Expression.* http://www. internationalpen.org.uk/go/freedom-of-expression. (Accessed 5th October 2010).

58. This Chapter has been developed from an article I wrote that was published in March 2010, and there are some overlaps here in terms of content and structure. Please see McRobie, Heather. 'Karadžić, Riefenstahl and Rushdie' in *Novi Pogledi* Vol 16. ACIPS, University of Sarajevo. 15th March 2010.

59 A comprehensive account of the international legal protection of freedom of expression can be found at the Human Rights Education Associates's website. http:// www.hrea.org/index.php?base_id=147. Interestingly, PEN International states on its website that it helped define the concept of freedom of expression that is now enshrined under Article 19 of the Universal Declaration of Human Rights. I will not, however, attempt to use international legal standards to 'determine' whether Karadžić's poetry should be banned, partly due to my focus here on political philosophy, and also due to the incompleteness of current norms of international law, which, in my view, often unjustifiably sideline the issue of gender and, particularly, the LGBT community, in the phrasing and scope of laws against incitement to violence, which are primarily written with 'incitement to racial hatred' in mind. In other words, part of the work still to be done on the issue of hate speech is a change in the legal parameters of what hate speech is.

60. For a fuller explanation of how hate speech performs this function, see Tsesis, Alexander. *Destructive Messages: How Hate Speech Paves the Way for Harmful Social Movements.* New York University Press. New York, USA. 2002.

61. In keeping with the widely-established tradition in literary criticism to keep separate the 'voice' of the author and the

actual voice or intentions of the writer of the poems, we cannot assume that Karadžić's poetry written from the first-person is necessarily his own 'voice' expressing his own views. We could, though, perhaps reassert Lionel Trilling's idea of sincerity of voice in modern literature, and argue that, when taken as a whole body of work and contextualized in Karadžić's own public life and his cultural context, we can assume that the themes and tone of his poetry provide insight into his worldview and his self-image.

62. Surdukowski, Jay. 'Is Poetry a War Crime? : Reckoning for Radovan Karadžić the Poet Warrior.' *Michigan Journal of International Law*, Vol 47. July 2005. p.9.
63. Surdukowski, p.6.
64. Surdukowski, p.12.
65. See Hudson, Robert. 'Songs of Seduction: Popular Music and Serbian Nationalism', *Patterns of Prejudice*, Vol 37, No 2. 2003.
66. Surdukowski, p.15.
67. Sontag, Susan. 'Fascinating Fascism.' *New York Review of Books*, Vol 22, No 1. Feb 1975.
68. Sontag, Susan. Ibid.
69. Bauman, Zygmunt. *Modernity and the Holocaust*. Cornell University Press. Ithaca, NY. USA. 1989.
70. Arendt, Hannah. *Eichmann in Jerusalem: A Report on the Banality of Evil*. Penguin reissued edition. London, United Kingdom. 1993.
71. Said, Edward. *Culture and Imperialism*. Vintage Press. London, UK. 1993.
72. Eagleton, Terry, Fredric Jameson and Edward Said. *Nationalism, Colonialism and Literature*. University of Minnesota Press. Minneapolis, USA. 1990.
73. Sontag, ibid.
74. Habermas, Jürgen. *Theory of Communicative Action*. Polity Press. Cambridge, United Kingdom. 1987.
75. It is worth noting that not all scholars are convinced by the

argument of contextualisation as a way of 'neutralising' the potency of artistic and literary hate speech. One obvious objection is the practical question of what measures it takes, exactly, to neutralise the original message of, say, Riefenstahl's films. Other scholars, however, maintain their position against 'contextualisation' even when they agree that this neutralisation will be effective. For instance, in October 2010 the renowned Holocaust historian Deborah Lipstadt supported the censorship of a 'contextualised re-working' of the Nazi film *Jud Süss* into the 2010 film *Jud Süss: A Film Without A Conscience*. The 2010 production works as a 'film within a film', whereby it re-enacts parts of the infamously anti-Semitic original film *Jud Süss*, of which Josef Goebbels was the producer, whilst also telling the 'backstory' (in fictionalised form) of the making of the original film. This backstory is fully intended to 'contextualise' the original *Jud Süss*, showing its overtly manipulative styling and malicious intent. Lipstadt, however, whilst recognising that this would disempower the message of the original film, still concurred with censors in 2010 who stated that the original film's content meant it should not be broadcast.

See: Lipstadt, Deborah. 'Even a 'remake' of *Jud Süss* can never be neutral.' *The Guardian* newspaper. 5th October 2010. Available online at http://www.guardian.co.uk/comment-isfree/2010/oct/05/jud-suss-goebbels-remake-germany. (Accessed 5th October 2010).

76. Nussbaum, Martha: *Frontiers of Justice: Disability, Nationality, Species Membership.* Harvard University Press. Cambridge, MA. USA. 2006. p.288.

77. Nussbaum, Martha. *Frontiers of Justice.* p.291.

78. Gelber, Katharine. *Speaking Back: the Free Speech versus Hate Speech Debate.* John Benjamin Publishers. Philadelphia, USA. 2002. p.8.

79. Gelber, Katharine.p.13.

80. Parekh, Bhikhu, 'Group Libel and Freedom of Expression: Thoughts on the Rushdie Affair' in Coliver, Sandra, ed. *Striking a Balance: Hate Speech, Freedom of Expression and Non-Discrimination.* London and Essex: ARTICLE 19 and Human Rights Centre, University of Essex. 1992. p.389.

81. Barry, Brian. *Culture and Equality: An Egalitarian Critique of Multiculturalism.* Cambridge MA: Harvard University Press. 2001. p.31.

82. Nussbaum, Martha. *Frontiers of Justice: Disability, Nationality, Species Membership. Harvard* University Press. Cambridge, USA. 2006. p282.

83. See: The Lady Chatterley Lover's Trial. *BBC News.* http://news.bbc.co.uk/onthisday/hi/dates/stories/november/10/newsid_2965000/2965194.stm (Accessed October 2nd 2010).

Contemporary culture has eliminated both the concept of the
public and the figure of the intellectual. Former public spaces –
both physical and cultural – are now either derelict or colonized
by advertising. A cretinous anti-intellectualism presides,
cheerled by expensively educated hacks in the pay of
multinational corporations who reassure their bored readers
that there is no need to rouse themselves from their interpassive
stupor. The informal censorship internalized and propagated by
the cultural workers of late capitalism generates a banal
conformity that the propaganda chiefs of Stalinism could only
ever have dreamt of imposing. Zer0 Books knows that another
kind of discourse – intellectual without being academic, popular
without being populist – is not only possible: it is already
flourishing, in the regions beyond the striplit malls of so-called
mass media and the neurotically bureaucratic halls of the
academy. Zer0 is committed to the idea of publishing as a
making public of the intellectual. It is convinced that in
the unthinking, blandly consensual culture in which we live,
critical and engaged theoretical reflection is more important
than ever before.